CHRISTMAS JARS

COOKBOOK

Other Books by
JASON F. WRIGHT

FICTION
Christmas Jars
The Wednesday Letters
Christmas Jars Reunion
Penny's Christmas Jar Miracle
The Seventeen Second Miracle
The Wedding Letters
Recovering Charles
Christmas Jars Journey
The James Miracle
The 13th Day of Christmas
Even the Dog Knows

NONFICTION
Until You Find Strength
Rise Today

CHRISTMAS JARS

COOKBOOK

Recipes, Crafts, and Heartwarming Stories from Our Family to Yours

JASON AND KODI WRIGHT

SHADOW
MOUNTAIN
PUBLISHING

Photography credit: Kodi Wright

Interior art credit: pgmart / Adobe Stock and rosinka / Adobe Stock

Library of Congress Cataloging-in-Publication Data
Names: Wright, Jason F. author | Wright, Kodi E. author
Title: Christmas jars cookbook : recipes, crafts, and heartwarming stories from our family to yours / Jason and Kodi Wright.
Description: [Salt Lake City] : Shadow Mountain Publishing, [2025] | Series: Christmas jars | Includes index. | Summary: "Authors Jason F. Wright and Kodi Wright offer recipes and crafts that can be made and gifted to others in the spirit of their Christmas Jars initiative. Includes journal pages that readers can use to chronicle their gifts"—Provided by publisher.
Identifiers: LCCN 2025006491 (print) | LCCN 2025006492 (ebook) | ISBN 9781639934270 hardback | ISBN 9781649334640 ebook
Subjects: LCSH: Christmas cooking | Christmas stories | LCGFT: Cookbooks Classification: LCC TX739.2.C45 W754 2025 (print) | LCC TX739.2.C45 (ebook) | DDC 641.5/686—dc23/eng/20250227
LC record available at https://lccn.loc.gov/2025006491
LC ebook record available at https://lccn.loc.gov/2025006492

Printed in China
Regent Publishing Services Limited, Hong Kong, China

10   9   8   7   6   5   4   3   2   1

To our grandchildren—those already here
creating beautiful chaos, and those yet to come.
We'll see you at Lolli and Pop Camp!

CONTENTS

CONTENTS

Caramel Apple Cheesecake Dip

If you're able to walk by the apple display at your local grocery store without imagining slicing them up and dipping them in caramel, then we don't even know who you are. And if you don't like caramel, cheesecake, or dip, why even celebrate the holiday season?

Top tip: Do not make this delectable dip if you don't already have apples on hand. What are you going to do? Eat it with a spoon straight from the pan? (Don't answer that.)

2 (8-ounce) packages cream cheese, chilled

1 cup caramel ice cream topping, chilled

1 to 2 packages graham crackers

Apples of your choice (Disclaimer: If you choose anything other than Granny Smith, the dessert warranty is voided.)

Whip the cream cheese until smooth and fluffy. This should take about one minute, or the length of time your toddler is quiet in church.

Stir in the caramel ice cream topping.

Crush graham crackers in a plastic bag with a rolling pin until no large chunks remain. If large chunks do remain, ask yourself if you're committed enough for this recipe.

Cut apples into wedges.

To serve, dip the apple in the caramel cheesecake mixture and then dip in crushed graham crackers. After watching someone take their first apple, wink at them and say, "How 'bout them apples?"

Gluten-free tip: Substitute regular graham crackers with a gluten-free option. Will it taste exactly the same? Not quite. Will your celiac or gluten-sensitive recipients love you more than ever? Absolutely.

Annie Lou's Air-Dry Clay Garland or Ornaments

If there's a more adorable granddaughter than our Annie Lou, we haven't met her. And we've met all the toddlers. These ornaments are almost as fun to make as a tea party with Annie. In fact, try making these while holding a tea party. Tiaras optional.

---

1 (2.5-pound) tub air-dry clay, such as Crayola (or similar)

Snowflake or star cookie cutter

Pencil

White cording

Stain or decorative glaze, brown

Pencil

Rolling pin

150-grit sandpaper

Heat the oven to 200 degrees F. Putting the clay in a low-temperature oven speeds up the drying process. If you don't want to use your oven, or if it's broken because your husband used it to dry out his bicycling pants, you can leave them out to dry overnight. (The ornaments, not the pants—they're donezo.)

Roll out the clay and cut out your shapes. Make a hole at the top of the shape with the end of a small paintbrush or a straw.

Place the shapes on a cookie sheet covered with parchment paper. Do not use parchment paper with historical significance, like the Bill of Rights. Why do you even own that?

If you choose to bake them, place them in the oven for 30–40 minutes, flipping them once at the 15–20 minute mark.

For this next step, please protect your work area with plastic or cardboard. We are not liable for any permanent damage to people, places, granite countertops, or IKEA furniture.

Use a small rag to dip into the stain or the glaze and wipe it over the surface of your shape. Fold the rag over and wipe off the excess.

After the stain or glaze has dried, use the sandpaper to lightly sand the edges and top to smooth out and lighten them a bit from the stain. If you like them more rugged, like a Hallmark movie cowboy, you don't need to sand them.

Tie them into a garland along the white cording and let (insert your favorite little person) deliver it to a friend or neighbor.

If you prefer ornaments, you can use the cording or ribbon to add a loop to each piece and turn them into—wait for it—ornaments.

 Soundtrack tip: "God Rest Ye Merry Gentlemen" by Annie Lennox (A Christmas Cornucopia, Island Records, 2010).

SPRING FAMILY
Holton, Michigan

God bless; God is good! I will be sharing the story that affected my brother's family of six in December 2023. As the holidays approached and excitement was settling in, it was five days before Christmas when devastation hit. Night approached and the clock struck midnight, and then their family home became engulfed in flames, claiming everything they ever cherished, including a couple of the family pets while two escaped the flames. By the grace of God, the family was spared their lives, and no one was hurt.

The family gathered in the front yard, felt the heat on their faces, and watched their newly purchased home burn to the ground. Everything was gone. The idea of losing everything was overwhelming. Family, friends, and members of the community all stepped up and did not let this family go without. Donation sites were established, and items started pouring in to help the family get back on their feet.

It was a couple days after the fire, and I came home from work to find a gift nestled up by my garage door. I scooped up the gift and placed it under my tree until I could make contact with my brother's family. My guess by weight and sound was someone had made a dinner menu and packed up noodles in a box with a couple jars of sauce. Once the hustle of the holidays was over, I made a visit to the hotel where they were temporarily staying. I told them what my guess was, and we all laughed. The card was perfectly written with a beautiful message from God inside but left by an anonymous giver. The family was in suspense as the gift was opened.

Carefully packed with pool noodles came a *Christmas Jars* book accompanied by a jar full of change. We all sat there appreciating the idea that someone collected and donated their change that they had saved up, and it pulled on our heartstrings. My brother took the jar to the window for better lighting as we all guessed how much change was in the jar. He turned around in disbelief, his face fell to the floor as the only words that seemed to come out of his mouth were, "OMG, you guys . . . you GUYS! No freakin' way!"

He turned the jar upside down and from the bottom you could see a wad of money bundled together. We were all in disbelief that what we thought were pasta noodles turned into a substantial financial donation. Even though the family had lost everything, one thing they gained a better perspective on was that tragic event restored humanity and humbled our entire family.

Personally, I can't remember the last time I was that excited watching someone else open a gift. This truly reinstated the meaning of Christmas. From this day forward, we will be spreading the word and participating in the Christmas Jars movement. God bless.

Chocolate Strawberry Christmas Tree Cookies

Big recipe name. Massive recipe taste. Making these requires some planning and acquiring ingredients you might not have around the pantry, but the extra legwork is worth it. These cookies will stand out among anything else your friends and neighbors receive during the holidays.

Top tip: Check your phone, charge if low—because when these beauties are done, you're going to want pics for all the socials, maybe even MySpace. If you prefer to go old school, dig out that Polaroid. Respect.

COOKIES

1 (12-ounce) bag dark green candy melts, such as Wilton (available from Walmart or Amazon)

1 (13-ounce) package chocolate sandwich cookies, such as Oreos

White icing (see below)

1 (16-ounce) container fresh strawberries, stems cut off

Toothpicks

Sprinkles

Candy stars

ICING

2½ cups powdered sugar

3 tablespoons heavy cream

ICING INSTRUCTIONS

Place powdered sugar in a bowl and add water by the teaspoon, whisking until you reach your desired consistency. What's that desired consistency? We strongly recommend roughly the thickness of toothpaste, but you do you.

INSTRUCTIONS

Melt the candy melts in a double boiler slowly, stirring occasionally.

Spoon a small amount of icing onto the top of each cookie. This will adhere the strawberry to the cookie base, just like the paste we all ate in elementary school—but this kind is actually edible.

Once the candy melts are fully melted, turn the heat to low. Using a toothpick inserted into the cut end, dip the strawberries in the melted candy.

Gently shake off excess coating. Using a second toothpick inserted into the bottom end of the dipped strawberry, carefully place the strawberry into the icing on the cookie. Use caution—this is culinary cosmetic surgery.

While the candy coating is still melty, decorate with sprinkles and add a candy star to the top. It should solidify in about 10 minutes. If you live in a desert climate— or an actual desert—it will take much less time.

Let the finished cookies set.

Packaging tip: After taking those pics we talked about, deliver quickly. While they're stunning to look at, these don't store well and are best enjoyed right after making. Put several on a small plate and deliver by hand. Seeing the recipients' reaction is almost as delicious as the cookies.

Christmas Movie Caramel Corn

A Christmas movie in the Wright home is not complete without this perfectly munchable treat. On one memorable night in December of 1994, just as the family prepared to watch *A Christmas Story*, Jason scavenged the pantry and realized we'd run out of brown sugar. He was so upset, he unplugged the VHS player and threw it into the backyard. Since then, we've maintained a two-year supply of all ingredients listed below.

Top tip: Of all the desserts in this book, this one might be the toughest to part with when complete. If you don't alert your intended recipients in advance and embrace personal accountability, you're likely to consume this before it cools.

10–11 quarts popped popcorn (10–12 ounces unpopped)

2½ cups brown sugar

1 cup light corn syrup, such as Karo

1 (4-ounce) stick butter, plus more for pan preparation

1 (14-ounce) can sweetened condensed milk, such as Eagle Brand

1 tablespoon vanilla extract

Waxed paper

Heat and mix brown sugar, corn syrup, and butter in a saucepan.

Bring to a boil and gradually add the sweetened condensed milk.

Cook until a very soft ball is formed when added to water. Remove from the stove and add vanilla. Mix well.

Pour over the popcorn and stir well until it sticks together like friends on a field trip.

Spread out over buttered waxed paper until cool.

Pairs with: This delicious caramel corn pairs well with your fingers. You'll be licking your fingertips until January, at which point a New Year's resolution might be wise.

Bev's Floral Snowman

There isn't much Kodi's marvelous mother, Beverly, enjoys more than watching her grandchildren (and, let's face it, son-in-law) attempt to build a snowman outside her window. No group of humans in world history have spent more time moving snow from one side of the yard to the other without actually making anything resembling a snowman. It's truly a gift.

A snowman from a thrift or craft store

1 (6-ounce) can white spray paint, such as Krylon

Black acrylic paint

1 (.5-ounce) tube wax metallic finish (such as Rub 'n Buff), optional

Natural pressed dried flowers (available through Amazon)

1 (8-ounce) bottle Mod Podge

Medium-size artist paintbrush (between size 6 and 10)

1 (12-ounce) spray can Mod Podge acrylic sealer

Spray-paint the snowman white.

If he or she has a hat, paint it black. If not, abandon this craft for today. Snowmen deserve better.

Once the paint is dry, paint over it with Rub 'n Buff to give it a more vintage look, if you choose.

Lay out your flowers so you can see all the colors and varieties.

Working in small areas around the snowman, brush on some Mod Podge and gently add the pressed flowers to the wet area. Then very gently brush Mod Podge over the top of the flower.

Be very careful with your brush, as the petals are delicate and easy to tear. Don't believe us? Ask to see the unreleased Wright family holiday videos of 1999.

After you've covered the entire snowman with petals, gently brush another layer of Mod Podge over it all. When dry, spray with acrylic sealer spray.

 Soundtrack tip: "Frosty the Snowman" by Bing Crosby (Christmas Classics, Capitol Records, 2007).

LAURIE TINSLEY
Westfield, Indiana

I began my Christmas Jar journey in 2005 while working at a bookstore. I came across the book, read it, and it changed my life.

I suddenly saw the value in giving back in small ways and anonymously to those who needed to be lifted up. I felt the need to share that experience with as many people as I could. My Christmas Jars journey spanned thirteen countries and all fifty states as I sought people from around the world to read the book and become part of the "change" movement—a movement that would change lives through the simple act of giving a Christmas Jar to someone in need.

We were changing lives one family, one person, one Christmas Jar at a time. At the end of my efforts, I have been directly or indirectly responsible for over 1,300 jars being given away to those in need. Others were now experiencing what I had experienced . . . learning to live with my eyes wide open to those around me who needed to be seen, loved, and given a sliver of hope.

My personal journey over the years has had a lot of heartbreak. I've dealt with things I never imagined, but this movement helped me get through it. I poured myself into helping others and as I did, I found I was healing myself.

The movement was like a pebble being thrown into the pond. The ripple effect of giving one jar led to so many others receiving jars. The "paying it forward" concept was never defined better than it was with Christmas Jars.

It's been almost twenty years. People continue to reach out every year to let me know they are filling their jar with someone in mind. It fills up my heart and gives me great joy knowing that twenty years later, people are still living with their eyes and ears wide open to the needs of others . . . especially in the world we live in today.

Corny's Crunch Cookies

Sure, we all appreciate Tony the Tiger, but where's the love for Cornelius "Corny" Rooster? Does *Tony* have a recipe in this book? No, no he doesn't. This dessert pays homage to the beloved cereal mascot who's lived in that tiger's shadow for far too long.

Top tip: Don't try describing this recipe to your friends and family. They won't get it, and you'll waste precious minutes that could be spent making Corny's Crunch Cookies. Just ask them to trust you.

Parchment paper

3 cups corn flakes cereal

6 ounces (about half a bag) butterscotch chips

3 tablespoons creamy peanut butter

Place a sheet of parchment paper on a cookie sheet.

Melt the butterscotch chips in a double boiler slowly, stirring occasionally, then add the peanut butter and mix well.

Pour the mixture over the corn flakes and continue mixing until every single flake feels included.

Put tablespoon-size scoops on the cookie sheet.

Put in a cool place like a fridge, igloo, or that photography darkroom you built back in 2020 and haven't used since 2021.

Packaging tip: Skip the red-and-green plastic containers and package these in an opaque tub. Draw a rooster or an ear of corn on the lid, leave on a friend's porch, and wait for a phone call.

Charlie's Smiley Star

This craft is inspired by a baby who smiles more than one of those yellow Walmart stickers. Charlie came into the world smiling, and we can confirm that as of publication, he hasn't stopped. This isn't some kind of grandparent bias; it's on the internet, where all truth lives.

Several straight-ish twigs harvested from a tree or bush

Hot glue gun and glue sticks

Dried flowers, evergreen pieces, cotton material, or baby's breath

Ribbon

Hemp twine

Cut or break five pieces of twig roughly the same length.

Make an upside-down *V* with two twigs and use a small dot of hot glue to hold the point of the *V* together.

Next, attach a twig about a third of the way down from the point to make an *A* (both sides of the twig should stick out—you're making a star). Use two small dots of hot glue to connect the *A* twig to the *V* twigs. If you think "*V* Twigs" sounds like the name of a cool 80s cover band, you're absolutely right. We should start one. Call us.

Connect the outside edges of the *A* twig with a twig to the opposite point of each *V* twig. Use a small dot of glue to hold each of those tips in place and a dot of glue where the twig intersects the *V* twig below the *A* cross-twig.

Stare at it and ask yourself, "Am I smiling like Charlie?" If not, find more twigs and start over.

Use a 12-inch length of hemp twine to make a loop around the top of the star for hanging.

To decorate the star, use some strips of cotton material, dried flowers, and ribbon to give it some pizazz.

 *Soundtrack tip: "Christmas Time Is Here" by the Vince Guaraldi Trio (*A Charlie Brown Christmas, Craft Recordings *rerelease, 2022).*

WRIGHT FAMILY MEMORY
Jason Wright

One of my favorite Christmas Jar stories was something of a trainwreck, which was appropriate because our target that year lived near an old rail line. She was a widow who'd been suggested by a mutual friend as the perfect jar recipient. We had several missionaries from our church at our home that afternoon, along with a few friends, and they all wanted to tag along.

We parked a few blocks away and made our way to the woman's front porch. I stepped up alone, and the rest of the gang watched from a spot where they could see me, but she wouldn't be able to see them. I knocked and jumped off

the porch, but the door opened faster than expected, and I crouched behind her pickup truck in the driveway. In the distance I heard my ace delivery team laughing and running away.

Crouched on my knees wondering when my knees started creaking, I watched the woman appear outside and look to her left and right. I hid lower and waited for her to spot the jar and return inside the house. But instead of a door opening and closing behind her, I

heard words that still ring in my ears. "I see you over there! Excuse me? What are you doing?"

As I remained hidden out of sight and wondering where my team had gone,

I explained the jar and the tradition. Eventually I stood up and we chatted for a while. "I think the author of that book lives around here," she said before I left.

"Yeah," I said with a sly smile, "I've heard that too."

This experience reminds me that each delivery has been so unique, and none have gone perfectly according to plan. But for me, that's what makes this twenty-year-old tradition so special. The deliveries, the details, the emotions, and the memories are as unique as the families who receive our Christmas Jars. And it's never really about the money, it's about the love.

Crispy Butterscotch Yummies

If you've never tried this version of Rice Krispies treats, you haven't been living. This simple twist on the classic, served alongside juice boxes at peewee soccer games since the dawn of time, will make you question everything.

Top tip: We don't call these Yummies—plural—for no reason. Eating just one of these will be more difficult than waking up your Uncle Dan after his Christmas brunch nap.

3½ cups puffed rice cereal, such as Rice Krispies

2 cups powdered sugar

2 cups peanut butter

1 (4-ounce) stick butter

1½ (12-ounce) bags butterscotch chips, such as Guittard

Waxed paper

Mix the cereal with the powdered sugar. If you spill the sugar, clean the counter with a freshly licked finger.

Melt butter and mix with peanut butter.

Combine these siblings and mix well.

Shape into marble-sized balls. If you don't remember playing marbles, ask someone in their fifties how big those are (about ½-inch).

Using a double boiler, melt the butterscotch chips.

Dip balls into the hot butterscotch, coat completely, lie on waxed paper. (Not you, the treats.)

 Soundtrack tip: "Deck the Halls" by Tenth Avenue North (Decade the Halls, vol. 1, Provident Music, 2017).

CASSIDY PALMER (REYNOLDS)
Sandpoint, Idaho

My two sons and I feel very blessed this holiday season! We have so many wonderful people in our lives who care about us and want to help us have a wonderful Christmas. Yesterday, the evening of December 12, 2023, we heard three loud knocks on our front door. Slightly startled, I looked out the peephole and didn't see anyone.

After opening the door, I saw a jar of money on the mat. It had a paper inside with the words *Christmas Jar* typed on it. With no one in view I picked it up, said "thank you" to anyone listening, went back inside, and closed the door. My kids were in awe of what had just happened. I handed them the jar and walked outside, curious to see if anyone was out there, or if my neighbors had received a jar at their front doors.

There were two people across the parking lot, and it looked like they were trying to hide behind a car. They obviously didn't want to be seen, so I went back inside, not wanting to spoil the magic and miracles of Christmas. My kids and I sorted through the money in the jar. While sorting the money, my youngest son said, "What if there is a hundred-dollar bill in there?" I thought *There's no way,* but to my surprise not only was there a hundred-dollar bill, there was a fifty, and multiple twenties, tens, fives, and ones along with over sixty-five dollars in change. It was unbelievable! When they got done counting, there was three hundred forty-two dollars in total! My kids and I were speechless; we were in shock. The only words we could find were, "We are so blessed." It was truly amazing!

For many years, I have been raising my kids on my own, and I work hard to provide them with a good life. When the holidays come around, it gets difficult to afford extra things that are needed or wanted. I try to budget my money wisely, and I do pretty well for the most part, even with the payments I make to the attorney I hired to help me during the custody dispute with my kids' dad. I have been able to pay all but $1,000 dollars of the $10,000 I owe him. It has been a long year of court dates and stress. Knowing how much I owe my attorney has made it hard for me to be able to buy my kids the things they really want for Christmas.

The Christmas Jar has given me the opportunity to not only get things my kids need, but also to pay it forward and buy a little something for some of the incredible people we have in our lives.

Since I don't know who to thank, I will thank you for helping to start this tradition in communities like mine. It really is a blessing that we will never forget.

Sending wishes for a very merry Christmas!

Dixie's Chocolate Dixies

We know what you're wondering. Was the name Dixie inspired by the Wrights' neighbor's dog when they lived on Mariner Lane in the fall of 2005? Yes, obviously. And when you taste these treats for the first time, you'll want to pause—paws?— and enjoy a moment of silence for that scrappy terrier.

Top tip: Unless you live alone, we recommend making these while everyone is asleep. Otherwise you'll run out of peppermint patties. (Trust us. We've seen things.)

½ cup butter	2 teaspoons vanilla
4 ounces unsweetened chocolate	1 ½ teaspoons baking powder
4 eggs	½ teaspoon salt
2 cups sugar	1 (17-ounce) bag peppermint patties, such as York
2 ½ cups flour	

Breathe deeply and heat the oven to 350 degrees F.

Melt and stir the butter and chocolate until they're best friends. Let mixture cool.

Beat eggs and sugar, then add to chocolate mixture.

Mix dry ingredients, but don't judge them for not being as interesting as the wet mixture. Everyone has a role to play. Combine dry and wet mixtures well.

Chill out for at least 30 minutes. (Also, let the dessert cool in the fridge or freezer.)

Roll dough into balls, then roll in powdered sugar, and arrange on a cookie sheet. Bake for 15–18 minutes and use this time to begin listing which friends and neighbors will receive your delicious gift.

The moment they come out of the oven, gently place a peppermint patty in the center and whisper, "For Dixie."

Let cool.

Packaging tip: In the highly unlikely event you have extra peppermint patties, unwrap them and add some to the plate.

Dandy Decoupage Trinket Dish

If you own an aloha shirt, dig it out of your closet and throw it on for this particular craft. No one cares if it fits—Jason still squeezes into one from high school, and we try not to judge him.

1 medium or large seashell

2-ply napkins with Christmas or fall seasonal designs

1 (8-ounce) bottle Mod Podge

White acrylic paint

Gold paint pen

Medium-size artist paintbrushes (between size 6 and 10)

Carefully paint the inside of the seashell with white paint. Let dry.

Separate your 2-ply napkin. You only need the piece with the design, but you may wad up the other piece and throw it at a nearby crafting partner or child.

Cut out a piece of the napkin that will fit nicely inside the seashell. You can cut it down into small pieces that fit together, or just one large piece that fits inside. Just be sure it fits into a single layer with no overlap.

Brush a coat of Mod Podge onto the inside of the shell.

Lay the napkin in the shell and gently press it down to the edges. Be careful to not leave bubbles or folded areas in the napkin.

Once smooth, gently brush on another layer of Mod Podge. Be careful not to brush too hard, or you'll rip the napkin with your brute strength. If this happens, blame all the vitamins you've been taking lately.

Allow to dry completely for approximately 24 hours. When dry, lift to your ear and listen for the ocean. If you hear crashing waves, take a nap and try again.

Finally, take the gold paint pen and paint around the edge of the shell.

This is the perfect gift to hold rings, paperclips, coins, or potpourri.

 Soundtrack tip: "Mele Kalikimaka (Hawaiian Christmas Song)" by Bing Crosby (The Voice of Christmas, Decca, 1998).

KID-FRIENDLY

Dressed in Chocolate Pants Pretzel Wreaths

If the pretzel wreaths of your childhood didn't wear chocolate pants, ask your mother why. Then, after you've made this recipe and experienced the wreaths' majesty, do your best to forgive her and turn the page. She did the best she knew how.

Top tip: Kids love things that wear pants, especially desserts. We recommend you allow the littles in your life to participate but put them on a wreath budget or they'll eat their weight in pants.

1 (12-ounce) package green candy melts, such as Wilton (available from Walmart or Amazon)

1 (16-ounce) bag mini pretzels, such as Rold Gold

Holiday sprinkles

Melt the candy melts in a double boiler. If your boiler was single last time you used it, offer genuine congratulations.

Lay waxed paper on the counter.

Dip the bottom of each pretzel in the candy dip and lay them out in a small wreath shape.

Place another layer on top of the first by dipping pretzels in the chocolate and overlapping them on top of your original wreath shape.

Repeat one more time so the finished wreath is made of three layers of pretzels. Do not attempt more than four. We love you, but no one is ready for that.

Repeat the process to make additional wreaths.

Before the chocolate sets up, sprinkle the wreaths with holiday sprinkles. Allow them to set up.

Soundtrack tip: "Oh Christmas Wreath" by All Together Now (Hope Sweetly Rings, 2019).

LINDA WERNER WILLIAMS
Parksley, Virginia

After reading *Christmas Jars* last year, I decided to do a jar to give away. My daughters and I have been the recipient of many blessings after a house fire and the death of their father at the age of forty-five several years ago. Reading *Christmas Jars* was so heartfelt that I knew I had to begin a new tradition for our family. I labeled a mason jar "C. J." and put it out on the kitchen counter. My girls are grown now and out on their own. I told them about the jar and shared the book. By Christmas morning, the jar was full.

We all scrambled for last-minute change in our pocketbooks and car trays. After my grandchildren (five and eight) had opened all their gifts, I asked them if they wanted to ride out for a few minutes. We live in a rural area and riding out is common practice here! I told them that we were going to play Santa Claus to someone we did not know, but thought they might enjoy getting a gift. A gift of a Christmas Jar.

I told them to look at the different homes down the street and pick one out. My grandson saw a very large newly built home all decorated for Christmas and said, "How about that one?" He's five and didn't quite get it yet! We passed by several prospects, but we finally agreed on a small simple home. It had a handicapped ramp and a walker on the porch. No sign of any holiday decorations.

I asked the kids if they wanted me to go run the jar up to the front door, but they said they wanted to do it. One carried the jar and the other carried a card. The envelope just said, "This Christmas Jar is for you!" Inside the card said, "May the miracle of Christmas be with you today." They ran up to the door with such excitement!

As they ran back in their Christmas PJs and cowboy boots and jumped back in the car, the front door opened. I had hoped to be gone by then, but we weren't. We began to drive off, and I told the kids to wave. The lady at the door waved, picked up the jar and card, hugged them both (the jar and card), and blew kisses. I told the kids, "Now that's Christmas! Making someone happy and not telling anyone what you did. Make it a secret."

My granddaughter said, "That was so fun. Can we do it next year?" I said, "Of course." We were all smiles. Now, there is a jar on the kitchen counter, "C. J.," ready for Christmas 2021.

Ginger's Cream Cookies

Trust us. You would know if you'd ever had these cookies. We've made them for many friends through the years, and the raves never stop. Family legend says this recipe can be traced back to Kodi's great-great-grandmother's neighbor's kid named Ginger. We can't confirm that, but we can't deny it either.

Top tip: Some gingersnap purists suggest skipping the frosting. This is a happy cookbook, so we won't disparage those people on these pages. But we implore you— please don't skip the frosting.

COOKIES

¼ cup butter

½ cup sugar

1 egg

½ cup molasses

½ cup hot water

2 cups flour

½ teaspoon salt

1 scant teaspoon ginger

½ teaspoon each nutmeg, cloves, and cinnamon

1 teaspoon soda

FROSTING

16 ounces (half a 32-ounce bag) powdered sugar

2 tablespoons butter

Milk, as needed

Heat the oven to 400 degrees F.

While preheating, send your family out on an errand that takes at least an hour. Tell them they'll thank you on their return.

Mix all ingredients together in a stand mixer fitted with the paddle attachment.

Chill the dough thoroughly.

Drop by teaspoons onto a cookie sheet.

Bake for 8 minutes. If your family returns early, lock all the doors and pretend you can't hear them knocking.

Allow cookies to cool on a wire rack.

Melt the butter in a saucepan. Add the powdered sugar in increments with just enough milk to make a thick icing. How much is just enough? Trust your gut.

Frost the cookies, take two for yourself, unlock the doors, and watch as the smell of Ginger's Cream Cookies stops your family in their tracks.

 Soundtrack tip: "Under the Tree" by Ed Sheeran (That Christmas, *Netflix, 2024).*

Go Nuts for Candied Pecans

Our family acknowledges that for some of you, candied pecans could be considered an acquired taste. Before making these for Christmas gifts, you might consider asking your friends and loved ones a probing but subtle question, such as, "Do you like candied pecans?" If they say no, ask why they hate the holidays.

Top tip: Did you know pecans can go bad? Of course you did. Be sure you're using fresh pecans for this dessert. Pecans freeze well, so don't be afraid to keep your leftovers for a second batch next month. (Or tomorrow.)

2 cups pecan halves	½ teaspoon vanilla extract
6 tablespoons brown sugar	1½ tablespoons water
1½ teaspoons cinnamon	2 teaspoons orange zest
½ teaspoon sea salt	

Line a cookie sheet with parchment paper or a silicone baking mat.

Add brown sugar, cinnamon, salt, vanilla, water, and orange zest to a skillet.

Place the skillet over medium heat. Heat the mixture, stirring often, until the brown sugar melts into a bubbling sauce. This should take about one minute.

Stir in pecans until they are coated in the mixture.

Cook, stirring the entire time, until the pecans appear candied and smell nutty. This takes two to three minutes. You could use this time to ask your teenagers if they did their homework. If they didn't, threaten to withhold the pecans.

As the pecans heat up in the pan, the sauce will slowly coat them and turn shiny. Watch closely so the pecans don't burn. If they do, you've lost all leverage on the homework gambit.

Transfer the candied pecans to the prepared baking sheet and spread them out in one layer.

Allow the pecans to cool down and break them up before serving.

Packaging tip: These look fantastic in small cellophane bags tied at the top with a red or green bow.

WRIGHT FAMILY MEMORY
Kodi Wright

Over the years, most of our Christmas Jar deliveries have been "drop and run." But one year we chose to hand-deliver a jar, and it was just as special! We were out driving around on Christmas Eve, trying to decide who our recipient would be. We were heavily engaged in conversation in the car discussing potential options when we saw a man on a bike. It was quite cold and most stores were closed, so he really drew our attention. We quickly wondered if this was the man we should give our jar to. As we followed at a distance, we noticed that he seemed to be carrying everything he owned on this old bike.

He didn't have much of a coat, and all of us were in agreement that he was the one. We turned around in an empty parking lot and tried to find our friend, but he seemed to have vanished. It was as if he had disappeared! We were feeling bummed about losing our target, when we all of a sudden saw him sitting on a bench in front of a gas station. We pulled in, parked, and piled out of the car to present him with our jar. We explained the story behind the jar and placed it carefully in his hands. Tears were streaming down his face, and he shared his story of trying to turn his life around. He was so thankful to be noticed by someone, especially on

Christmas Eve, when he felt so very alone. The entire family left with tears in our eyes, and hope in our hearts that this man felt even a little bit of love from the Wrights in the form of a simple Christmas Jar.

Everyone's Favorite Embroidery Hoop Ornaments

Have you seen an embroidery hoop Christmas ornament in another craft book? Forget you ever saw it—this one has been scientifically proven to be the best in its class. Why else would it be called "Everyone's Favorite"? We're not bragging; it's Sewing Science 101.

4-inch embroidery hoops (as many as you want to make into ornaments)

#20 natural polished hemp twine

Small pine twigs

Individual holly berries

Wooden square letter beads (available at Michaels, Hobby Lobby, or through Amazon)

Hot glue gun and glue sticks

Lay out short holiday phrases with the wooden letters—like "Merry Christmas," "First Noel," "Happy Holidays," "Hallelujah," or "Who Ate All the Fudge?"

Cut your string in sections long enough to overlap your 4-inch hoop. Make it long enough that you will be able to pull the string taut and tie it in the back, but not so long that it reaches the moon. Be realistic.

String one word on each string.

Open the embroidery hoop and lay the string with the letters inside, with the extra string overlapping.

Place the outside ring over the top, keeping the strings straight.

Once you have the strings straight and the hoop fully back together, pull gently until tight.

If you placed two strings in the hoop, then carefully tie the two strings together and hot glue them down into the crevice of the hoop on the back side. As you do this, it's OK to laugh at the word *crevice*.

If you only have one string, hot glue it down in the crevice of the hoop on the back side.

At the top of the hoop, hot glue two pine twigs and two or three holly berries.

Delivery tip: This is a fun gift to deliver anonymously. Visit your neighbor and ask to borrow a cup of brown sugar or a small bag of cash. When they leave the room, place the ornament on their tree and smile knowing they'll spend a lifetime wondering who their secret Santa was.

Heaven's Peanut Butter Blossoms

These aren't just cookies, they're blossoms from heaven. When the Wright kiddos were still, well, kiddos, these Peanut Butter Blossoms had peacemaking power. There was no dispute, disagreement, or basement wrestling match that couldn't be resolved with this perfect marriage of chocolate and peanut butter.

Top tip: Don't scan the ingredients and ask yourself if you can cheat by using a name-brand peanut butter cup instead of milk chocolate Kisses. You can't. Don't mess with heaven. Your conscience will know—and so will the Wrights.

¾ cup creamy peanut butter

½ cup unsalted butter, softened

½ cup granulated sugar

½ cup light brown sugar

¼ teaspoon salt

1 large egg, room temperature

1 teaspoon vanilla extract

1½ cups all-purpose flour

½ teaspoon baking soda

36 milk chocolate Hershey Kisses (about half a 10-ounce bag), unwrapped

Heat the oven to 375 degrees F.

While lining a cookie sheet with parchment paper, ask yourself why we call them cookie sheets if they're good for baking other things. It feels wrong, yet we persist.

Combine the peanut butter, unsalted butter, sugars, and salt in the bowl of a stand mixer fitted with the paddle attachment.

Cream together by beating on medium speed until well mixed.

Add the egg and vanilla and beat until it looks like something you'd serve an angel.

Scrape the sides of the bowl. Leave no batter behind!

Add the flour and baking soda and beat on low speed until you arrive at mixing nirvana.

Scoop the dough and roll into 1-inch balls. Place on the cookie sheet roughly two inches apart. Cookies are like Kason and Koleson in the back seat: "He's touching me!"

Bake 8–10 minutes, or until the cookies look puffy and cracked, and the bottoms have just started to turn brown.

Immediately press a chocolate Kiss into the center of each cookie. The cookies will crack but embrace it. Baking is, after all, a metaphor for life.

Allow the cookies to cool completely on the pan until the chocolate is set.

 Soundtrack tip: "Christmas Kiss" by Steven Curtis Chapman (Joy, Reunion, 2012).

CINDY SCHMIDT
Columbus, Ohio

It's been a rough few years for me—loss, death, sickness, conflict, job loss, divorce, the pandemic. I suddenly developed several health issues that literally sidelined me for four months. Rarely went to work, missed events, and ruined holidays. I was sick and it was complicated. I am normally a very upbeat person, but I was sinking into despair day by day.

We came home late on Christmas Eve to find a gift tucked in our screen door. I thought, *Oh so sweet, a neighbor has left cookies or treats!* The bag was *very* heavy, and I opened it to find a jar brimming with coins and bills. There was a beautiful card about Jesus seeing me and loving me. I sat shocked and amazed; the jar is still by the couch. I have never seen such a gift. We are not rich people but far from poor—needy in some ways, but I felt maybe embarrassed to receive such a gift. There was over $1,000 in cash and probably $200 in coins. So extravagant. I cry every time I think of it.

That jar feels almost sacred—a gift from the Lord. I'm still sick (maybe seeing a glimmer of hope) but my heart is full, and I will indeed pass along a jar next Christmas. Just unbelievable!

I think the hardest part for me is that "I'M THE GIVER!" I send the cards, I give the gifts, I send the meals! I will help you all day long, but don't you dare try to help me! This fall I've been sick then sick then sick, and I've been so humbled. My small group came over (against my wishes!) and put up our

Christmas decorations! And then the Christmas Jar—the Lord is teaching me humility, and I'm learning to accept kindness. Thanks for your sweet book and the ripples of joy and wonder it brings!

Jadi's Happy Rolo Pretzels

-FRIENDLY

Anyone who's ever met Jadi knows that pretzels and Rolos are her happy place. When she was a precocious toddler, she once asked, "If there are no pretzels and Rolos in the next life, is heaven real?"

Top tip: These are best made with square pretzels, but for reasons beyond all human comprehension, not all stores carry them. Substitute with the smallest snack-size option you can find.

1 (16-ounce) bag square pretzels, such as Snyder's of Hanover Snaps

1 (36-ounce) bag chocolate caramel candies, such as Rolos

1 (38-ounce) bag red and green candy-coated chocolate candies, such as M&M's Christmas Gift, or substitute

Heat the oven to 250 degrees F.

Place a piece of parchment paper on a cookie sheet and cover in a single layer of pretzels.

Place one unwrapped Rolo on top of each pretzel. If not perfectly centered, pick up the Rolo and try again. If still not centered, or if anything feels even remotely off, pick up the Rolo and eat it. Repeat placement procedure.

Bake for 3–5 minutes, but don't wander far. You want the Rolos soft, not melted into a sea of caramel. (If this happens, find a spoon and tell no one.)

Remove from the oven and place a single red or green M&M on top of the Rolo and press down gently.

Let cool.

Soundtrack tip: "Jingle Bell Rock" by Kelly Clarkson (When Christmas Comes Around . . . Again, Atlantic, 2024).

CHRISTMAS JARS COOKBOOK

June's Foolproof Fudge

Kodi's beloved Aunt June perfected this simple recipe over decades of practice. Its texture is so silky smooth, your tastebuds will think you're listening to the "Jazz in the Background" playlist on Spotify.

Top tip: We call this foolproof, but that never stops Jason from eating half the marshmallow creme. Consider keeping an extra jar under lock and key.

1 (12-ounce) can evaporated milk

2 tablespoons butter

4 ½ cups sugar

1 dash salt

1 (12-ounce) bag (2 cups) semisweet chocolate chips

3 (4.4-ounce) milk chocolate bars, such as Hershey's XL Bar, broken into pieces

1 (13-ounce) jar marshmallow creme, such as Jet-Puffed

Bring this tasty concoction to a rigorous boil. Stir often. Then, just when it seems as though the ingredients are debating whether *Top Gun* is a Christmas movie or not, reduce heat and let simmer for six minutes.

Slowly pour over the chocolate chips, the chocolate bar pieces, and the marshmallow creme.

Beat until the chocolate melts. Then, when no one is looking, plunge your index finger into the bowl and taste. If you hear angels, you're nearly done.

If you're a fudge purist—furist?—leave as is and pour the mixture into a buttered pan. If you're feeling adventurous, consider stirring in chopped walnuts, almonds, or mini marshmallows.

Store in a cool place and when solid, cut into small pieces.

Packaging tip: Pieces fit nicely in cellophane bags. Seal with a small sticker or holiday bow.

WRIGHT FAMILY MEMORY
Jadi Wright

One Christmas Eve, we were all out on the hunt for someone to give our jar to when we found ourselves at a truck stop in a neighboring town. We spotted a truck driver traveling alone during the holidays. We felt compelled to talk to him, and we asked his name and his story. He told us he was working during the holidays and missing his family back home.

Even at a young age, I could tell he was a hardworking and kind man. We explained our tradition, gave him our Christmas Jar, and encouraged him to buy some gifts for his family. He expressed his sorrow to be away from his family and his gratitude for this act of kindness. He told us that while the money was a blessing, what he really needed was the moment of human connection and the sense of belonging. I remember how privileged and blessed I felt to be with my family that Christmas. I remember how amazing it felt to know we didn't glance over someone that could benefit from our kindness. I learned of the inherent worth of each person I cross paths with, and of the capacity we hold to love a stranger. That particular Christmas Jar taught me that I have the power to make someone feel loved and seen, often with just a simple gesture.

Troy's White Chocolate Cinnamon Sugar Pretzels

Raise your hand if you think white chocolate doesn't get enough love when it comes to holiday baking. (Hand down, son-in-law Troy. We already know you love white chocolate almost as much as you love Oakli. We've been getting your DMs.) This creation is among the most likely to inspire your friends to ask for the recipe. You can share it, of course, or lovingly invite them to buy their own copy of this book.

Top tip: Any recipe that calls for one bag of pretzels really means two—one for the recipe and one to snack on. It's not controversial; it's just the snack cycle of life.

1 (16-ounce) bag mini pretzels, such as Rold Gold Tiny Twists

⅔ cup oil

⅓ cup sugar

1½ teaspoons cinnamon

1½ cups cinnamon sugar, for sprinkling

1 cup white chocolate chips, or white chocolate melts

Whisk oil, sugar, and cinnamon together in a large microwave-safe bowl.

Add pretzels and stir until coated.

Microwave for 50 seconds, stir, then microwave again for 40 seconds. Be aware: This gives you enough time to check your notifications, but not enough to scroll.

Carefully dump the pretzels onto two cookie sheets covered with parchment paper.

While still hot, sprinkle with cinnamon sugar mixture.

As pretzels cool, melt white chocolate in a double boiler.

Drizzle over pretzels and let the white chocolate set up before serving or bagging up.

 Gluten-free tip: Substitute regular pretzels for a gluten-free option. As Jason or any GF consumer will tell you, everything that's manufactured to be gluten-free tastes much better dipped in, drizzled with, or soaked in chocolate.

Kason's Colossal Cookies

Everything about these cookies is colossal. Their size, their taste, their love of 2000s rap. Let's face it, Kason chose to include this recipe because he's hoping a loyal reader will make a batch and drop them at his front door. Smart guy!

Top tip: This is one of the most filling cookies you'll ever devour. On the day you make these, we suggest canceling dinner.

3 eggs

1¼ cups brown sugar, packed

¾ cup white sugar

2 teaspoons vanilla

1 teaspoon honey

1 (4-ounce) stick butter, softened

13.5 ounces (¾ an 18-ounce jar) creamy peanut butter

4⅓ cups gluten-free oats

5 ounces (½ bag) each peanut butter chips, such as Reese's; semisweet or milk chocolate chips, such as Nestlé, and red-and-green mini chocolate candies, such as M&M's—or substitute any other favorite small, tasty candies

Heat the oven to 350 degrees F.

Mix all ingredients together and skip the gym. You just rocked arm day.

Using an ice cream scoop, place dough balls on a cookie sheet 3 inches apart.

Bake 10–12 minutes. Immediately after removing the cookie sheet from the oven, grab a cookie, nearly drop it, then toss it carefully between your hands half a dozen times.

Take a bite and sputter out the phrase, "Oh! Hot! Hot! So hot! So good!"

Allow other cookies to cool.

Pairs with: These cookies pair nicely with a tall glass of milk.

MILLER FAMILY
Edinburg, Virginia

It has been four weeks since Thanksgiving. My and my family's lives have forever been changed. We lost our house and most of our belongings to devastating fires. (Yes, it burned twice.) Standing there both days, I wondered how we would ever recover.

We spent the next two weeks in a motel. We learned many things in those two weeks.

First and most importantly, the physical belongings—while upsetting to lose the memories—they don't really matter. What matters is our loved ones. The four of us have become closer and our bond stronger.

Second, we learned that family is not limited to blood. Our blood family has been there offering everything they could. And so has our work, school, and fire department family. While we knew we had many friends, we found out it is a big family.

Then there is the community. We have had complete strangers stop us in town and offered their sympathy for our loss. If it was not for this loss, I would not know how lucky we are.

Many would wonder how I can say we are lucky. If it wasn't for losing our house and having every vehicle we own break down in the last month, we would not know how much we are loved and cared for.

There are so many people to thank that it has been overwhelming. If you have given to us in any way, please know if we have not said it to you, we are thankful and will never be able to truly repay those who have helped us. The best we can do is try to pay it forward.

We were the recipients of a Christmas Jar. We have taken that jar and are working on filling it for someone next year. This jar is a physical reminder to us to treasure what we have now as it can all be gone in a flash. For those that are wondering, we are in a house that will be our home until we rebuild.

Through the generosity of many people, we have been able to fully furnish it with minimal purchases. We have been able to make it not just a house but a home. We were able to meet our goal of being in a house for Christmas. We had several groups that helped our family to have a wonderful Christmas.

Again, we thank those who were generous with presents and love. We thank God for showing us what we truly have and how loved we are by family, friends, and community. As I have come to understand, it is only up from here.

May 2021 be a better year for us all.

Kodi's Level-Up S'mores Cookies

Everyone has their favorite cookie recipe, but not everyone has a recipe capable of leveling up your family, work, or church Christmas party. These cookies are so good, other cookies on the dessert table will accuse them of bullying.

Top tip: This recipe requires greater attention to detail than many others in this collection. We strongly suggest you not undertake Kodi's Level-Up S'mores Cookies without a full night's sleep and a healthy breakfast.

1 cup salted butter

¾ cup granulated sugar

¾ cup light brown sugar, packed

2 teaspoons vanilla

2 eggs

2¼ cups + 2 tablespoons all-purpose flour

1 teaspoon baking soda

1 teaspoon salt

2 cups semisweet chocolate chips

1 (10-ounce) bag mini marshmallows

2 (12-ounce) packages milk chocolate candy melt wafers, such as Wilton (available from Walmart or Amazon)

1-2 packages (¼ to ½ 14.4-ounce box) graham crackers, crushed

Waxed paper

Heat the oven to 375 degrees F. and line a cookie sheet with parchment paper.

Cream together butter and sugars in a stand mixer fitted with the paddle attachment. Or, if you prefer, you can sit.

Add the eggs one at a time, mixing thoroughly between each addition.

Add vanilla and mix well.

Add the flour, baking soda, and salt. Mix until a soft dough forms. You might want to take a pinch and taste this. Or maybe don't. Salmonella's still a thing, right?

Add in the chocolate chips and mix until evenly distributed.

Drop rounded tablespoons of dough onto the prepared cookie sheet.

Bake for 5 minutes.

Unless you have comically long arms and shoulder-length fire-resistant gloves, remove the pan from the oven and add mini marshmallows on top of each cookie.

Return to the oven and bake just long enough to brown the marshmallows. Watch this step closely, or you'll burn the marshmallows. You could even burn the cookies—and if you do, your life won't be the same again.

When the marshmallows are browned, remove from the oven and let sit for 1 minute before transferring to a cooling rack. If you don't own a cooling rack, you should have asked your neighbors in advance. We warned you not to take this recipe lightly.

After all the batches are baked, melt the chocolate wafers in a double boiler.

Crush the graham crackers and place them in a bowl.

Place waxed paper on a cookie sheet.

Dip each cookie in the melted chocolate until half the cookie is covered, then sprinkle with the crushed graham crackers.

Place each dipped and sprinkled cookie on the waxed paper and let sit until the chocolate sets.

Packaging tip: When gifting these cookies, be careful not to obscure their appearance. Consider using small plates with clear plastic wrap. Recipients will wonder whether to eat them or put them in a shadow box for display.

KID-FRIENDLY

GLUTEN
FREE

Koleson's Cashew Bark

Picture yourself on an early-evening hike in a gorgeous forest filled with sumptuous chocolate trees. Now imagine stopping, peeling off a piece of bark, and taking a nibble.

Tasty, right? That's Koleson's cashew bark in a nutshell. (See what we did there?)

Top tip: This recipe is kid-friendly with supervision. Young dessert makers will especially enjoy breaking up the chocolate after it's cooled.

1 (24-ounce) package chocolate almond bark candy coating, such as Great Value

3 cups cashews

Waxed paper

Place almond bark in a saucepan and melt over very low heat. Stir until the chocolate is smooth and velvety, like a 1950s thrift-store men's suit.

Stir in the cashews and spread the heavenly mixture on waxed paper in a thin layer.

Using a spoon, or chopsticks if you're as adventurous as Koleson, pick up and eat a single chocolate-coated cashew. If it makes your heart happy, you've done your job.

Lastly, wait until the rest of the batch cools. Break the bark into small pieces.

Packaging tip: These look terrific in small cellophane bags. As you package them, be sure to "accidentally" break the larger pieces and eat what doesn't quite fit.

WRIGHT FAMILY MEMORY
Koleson Wright

My favorite Christmas Jars story happened in the Walmart parking lot on Christmas day. This was unusual for many reasons, but mostly because we don't usually give our jars away on Christmas Day. Christmas is a busy day for most, including us, so we usually give our jars out on the 24th, just like in Dad's book.

We didn't have anyone in mind to give our jar to, and the day came and went. So, on Christmas Day, we brainstormed a final time on who would receive it. We struggled to come to a consensus. Then someone suggested giving it to someone who had to work on Christmas. We all felt good about that, and we had the perfect person in mind.

At the time, our Walmart was open 24/7 every single day except Christmas. Because of this, they took the opportunity to have a street sweeper come and sweep the parking lot that day because it was the only time of the year that there would be no cars around. So we knew that there would be someone—all alone on Christmas—driving a street sweeper around the Walmart parking lot. Having a plan, we drove over to Walmart, flagged down the driver, and handed over the jar.

This happened many years ago, and to be honest, I don't remember all the details very well. But looking back, it makes me happy that we were able to brighten someone's Christmas. I hope that we were able to remind them that they aren't alone. What they ended up doing with the change in the jar wasn't important. Because it's not about money. It's about being seen. Being acknowledged. I probably didn't understand that at the time; I'm sure I was begging to go home to get my Christmas gifts. But looking back, that experience is what helped me realize what the Christmas Jar is all about.

Grandma Sarah's Wooden Ring Garland

This cherished craft comes from Kodi's great-great-great-great-great-grandmother. We don't have her permission to publish this because she's fictional, but we're including it anyway because this garland is a holiday game changer. (RIP Grandma Sarah.)

13–15 (2- to 3-inch) natural wooden rings (available at Michaels, Hobby Lobby, or through Amazon)

Black acrylic paint

Any Christmas craft embellishments such as ribbon, wooden cube letters, mini pine twigs, holly berries, etc.

Black grosgrain ribbon

Hot glue gun and glue sticks

Paint the wooden rings black with the acrylic paint and allow to dry.

Decorate each ring with the Christmas craft embellishments. You could wrap a colorful ribbon around a ring and secure the ends with hot glue.

You could decorate several rings with short Christmasy words such as "Noel," "Yule," "Joy," "Elf," "Snow," or "Star." String your words together and hot glue one end to the ring, wait for it to set up, pull the string taut and hot glue the other end to the other side of the ring.

You could hot glue a small pine sprig and holly berries to a few more rings.

Using a couple of mini pinecones, you could hot glue them to the top of a ring and secure them with a dot of glue.

You could make a ribbon bow and hot glue it to the top of the ring.

Once all the rings have been made, connect them with black grosgrain ribbon by cutting 4½-inch-long pieces, and connecting two rings with a loop of ribbon secured in the back with a dot of hot glue. Continue connecting rings until you have a long chain.

Cut two 12-inch-long pieces of ribbon for each end, wrap them around an end ring and secure with a dot of hot glue, making a loop to hang the garland.

Naughty Knotty Yeast Rolls

We used to call these Knotty Yeast Rolls. But when Jason was diagnosed with celiac disease in 2014, these became very, very naughty. All these years later, anytime Kodi makes these delicious smelling rolls for dinner, Jason excuses himself and weeps softly as he circles the neighborhood in his car.

Top tip: You could try replacing the flour with a gluten-free alternative, but as of publication, we've not found a suitable replacement for this particular recipe. So while Jason misses these rolls dearly, he personally prefers to reminisce on their memory rather than settle for a subpar GF alternative.

1 (¼-ounce) package active dry yeast	2 large egg whites, room temperature, beaten
1 cup 2% milk	1 teaspoon salt
¼ cup raw honey	3½ to 4 cups all-purpose flour, divided
¼ cup unsweetened applesauce	Nonstick cooking spray

Warm milk to 110 to 115 degrees F. Mix in honey, and using a large bowl, dissolve yeast in milk and honey mixture. Allow to get frothy (about 5–15 minutes), then add applesauce, egg whites, salt, and two cups of flour.

Beat until smooth and stir in enough remaining flour to form a soft dough.

Turn out onto a lightly floured surface and knead until smooth and elastic. This should take 6–8 minutes, one for every time Kodi caught Koleson snooping in her closet for Christmas presents.

Place dough in a bowl coated with nonstick cooking spray and expect that the dough will still be slightly sticky. Sticky fingers, counters, and couch cushions are bad. Sticky dough is good.

Flip dough over so the top is equally coated with cooking spray.

Cover and let rise for about an hour, or until it doubles in size. If the dough gets to the size of Jason's ankle after he and Jadi fell down the stairs in December 2003, it's too big.

Turn out dough onto a lightly floured surface and divide into 24 pieces. Shape each portion into an 8-inch-long rope and tie into a knot.

Line two half-sheet baking pans with parchment paper. Heat the oven to 375 degrees F.

Cover and let rise until doubled in size. This should take approximately 30 minutes, enough time to make a long list of potential recipients of a Naughty Knotty Yeast Roll—and to edit it down to whatever might be left after your family gets their hands on them first.

Bake for 12–16 minutes or until golden brown. Place on cooling racks and express your gratitude to the spirit of the baking that you aren't allergic to gluten.

Pairs with: These rolls pair well with Santa's Strawberry Jam on page 98. A warm basket of rolls and a jar of jam does more than make your neighbor happy—you might find your name in their will.

MAUREEN BROWN
Bumpass, Virginia

I received a Christmas Jar. We are an elderly couple who moved back to Louisa, Virginia, in 2018 to be closer to our doctors and downsize to a small house I could more easily manage. In 2015, my husband survived a sudden cardiac arrest resulting in brain damage and loss of his job. In 2019, I required heart surgery myself.

We love our house and bought it with a home inspection which will become ironic as our story unfolds. 2020 began with my husband having a second cardiac arrest, and during the heart surgery, the anesthesia caused more brain damage and psychotic behavior. He became delusional, combative, hallucinating, and suicidal and they treated him with powerful medications to no avail.

The gentle quiet man I had loved as my husband for forty-six years had become an angry despondent stranger. It's just the two of us with no children or family. On a fixed income, I am his sole caregiver 24/7. So for ten months, chaos ensued—911 calls, EMTs, and police; it was heartbreaking. Then I took things in my own hands and said, "Enough. These meds are what is causing this."

I found a doctor who agreed to get him off the meds, and now he is my husband again, albeit brain-damaged with no memory, but life was peaceful . . . until that house inspection. 2020 has given us a complete septic system overhaul, water line replacement from the well to the house, three dead appliances, completely new and upgraded electrical panel (as it was insufficient and not even grounded), eight inches of water in the crawl space from rain, and then a drain pipe installed under and out of the crawl space. Then the week we received the Christmas Jar, the entire HVAC system quit.

I was beyond the end of my rope financially and did not know how to get through the next few months. I know a tax return will give us some relief, but that's months away. And I no longer have my beloved partner to discuss this with as his brilliant mind has left me, but still so grateful for his still being here. When I saw the bag on our porch, I thought a neighbor had left cookies. Then when I saw the jars of coins and the book, I could not believe someone would be this kind.

We stayed to ourselves. I have no time other than to care for him. I did not empty the jars until that night and when the hidden currency tumbled out with the coins, I was so humbled and shocked I cried happy tears . . . and some sad tears because I could not thank the person myself. So I prayed to God to please bless them and hold them close. Throughout my life I have found it difficult to ask for help, but an angel did the asking for me and my Christmas Jar was the answer.

Not Your Grandma's Sugar Cookies

There are sugar cookies, and then there are *sugar cookies*. This particular recipe creates a cookie so delicious you'll be tempted to call, text, or FaceTime your grandmother and apologize for your tastebud disloyalty. This never-before-published recipe has been in Kodi's family for so long, there are rumors the cookies were first made for King Charles I in 1649 as his last meal. Hard to prove, we know—just go with it.

Top tip: Every sugar cookie tastes better when it's shaped like a Christmas ornament, bell, or eight-foot toboggan. Before diving into Not Your Grandma's Sugar Cookies, consider making a trip to your local dollar store to find some creative cookie cutters.

COOKIES

1 cup buttermilk

1 cup sugar

1 cup shortening, melted

2 eggs

1 teaspoon vanilla

4 cups flour

1 teaspoon baking soda

3 teaspoons baking powder

1 teaspoon salt

FROSTING

1 (4-ounce) stick butter

4 tablespoons milk

Powdered sugar

Food coloring, as desired

INSTRUCTIONS

Heat the oven to 350 degrees F.

Mix all ingredients together to make a stiff dough.

Roll out dough on a floured board and cut into your desired shapes. This is a great chance to get the littles involved, because there's a chance they'll be bored and disappear before it's time to frost.

Bake until the edges start to brown, usually about 10 minutes.

Place cookies on a cooling rack to, you know, cool.

FROSTING INSTRUCTIONS

While the cookies cool, melt the butter in a saucepan and stir in the milk. Remove from heat and slowly add powdered sugar until the frosting is a spreading consistency.

Consider using a piping bag to frost and decorate your cookies. If the kids or spouses have returned to the kitchen, tell them they have to be licensed to use the piping bag and that the office is closed for the holidays. We've seen that work.

Otherwise, let all happy hands decorate and be prepared for someone to squeeze the remaining contents of all bags into his or her mouth. (It's Jason. It's always Jason.)

Packaging tip: Avoid plastic or foil that can stick to the fresh frosting and try delivering them immediately to your recipients on simple, uncovered plates. These aren't show cookies—they're meant to be eaten as soon as possible.

WRIGHT FAMILY MEMORY
Oakli Wright Van Meter

It was the day after Christmas when we learned of a family in our town whose home had burned down on Christmas Day. Dad reached out to the hotel where they were staying, and we arranged to go meet the family in the lobby and give them our Christmas Jar.

When we handed them the jar, there wasn't a single dry eye in the room. We were blessed that Christmas to be joined by my Grandma Sandi, and she shed many tears that day. She still talks about the experience often.

What a cool thing, too, for the employees working the front desk that night to witness this movement firsthand. It's not often that a third party gets a front-row seat to that special moment. Getting to see not only this family's gratitude for the jar itself, but also their gratitude for being seen and loved by their community. It's not often something you get to see when working the

hotel front desk, and I'm sure it's a memory they also won't forget.

I've participated in many Christmas Jar drop-offs over the years, and they often look different. Sometimes it's a ding-dong ditch and running off into the night. Sometimes it's choosing a random stranger at a gas station or in the grocery store who just seems like they need a spark of hope. And that's truly the magic of the movement. There is no right or wrong way to give a jar. It's not about the size of the jar or the number of coins inside. It's ultimately about bringing joy and hope to others. One of the reasons that this story has always stuck with me is there was so much hope in that hotel lobby. We felt it, the family receiving the jar felt it, and I'm sure those employees standing behind the desk that night felt it, too.

Nutty Nut Clusters

When most people think of slow cookers, they imagine stews, chili, and Sloppy Joes. Not the Wrights. We think of desserts. (Disclaimer: After making this concoction, you might never want to use your slow cooker for anything else. Consider buying a second.)

Top tip: If you have a nut allergy, or someone in your home has a nut allergy, or someone in your child's school has a nut allergy, and you were planning on sending Junior to school with a plastic tub packed with Nutty Nut Clusters, why are you torturing yourself? Turn the page.

1 (16-ounce) jar unsalted peanuts

1 (16-ounce) jar lightly salted peanuts

2 (10-ounce) bags peanut butter chips

1 (11.5-ounce) bag milk chocolate chips

1 (12-ounce) bag semisweet chocolate chips

2 (12-ounce) bags white chocolate candy melts, such as Wilton (available from Walmart or Amazon)

Plug in your slow cooker. This is more important than you might realize. Oakli tried making these once without plugging in her slow cooker and they didn't finish cooking until July.

Fill the bottom of the pot with the peanuts.

Layer on the peanut butter chips.

Layer on the milk and semisweet chocolate chips.

Layer the white chocolate candy melts on top.

Set the slow cooker to low and cook for one hour.

During this hour, find a family scrapbook and look at baby pictures of your children. Let the nostalgia wash over you until you're crying and wishing you owned a flux capacitor and a DeLorean.

Remove the lid and stir the pot, but not the way your cousin Darryl does at family picnics.

Replace the lid and cook for an additional 30 minutes.

Remove the lid once more and stir a final time.

Drop tablespoon-size clusters on a cookie sheet lined with parchment paper. Allow to cool for several hours before serving or sharing.

 Soundtrack tip: Cherie Call's entire Christmas album Gifts *(2008).*

Hope's Mini Decorative Wreaths

Picture everyone you know named Hope. Now forget them all and imagine Jeni Ross. The lovely Canadian actress played Hope in the film adaptation of *Christmas Jars*, and this craft is named for the character we've come to know and love.

Top tip: Feeling like this craft has met its match with your all-pro crafting skills? When you're done, send a photo of your creation to pics@christmasjars.com and I'll personally share your pics with Jeni.

Faux cypress napkin rings—or evergreenery to make wreaths yourself

Green floral wire, if making wreaths yourself

Mini gold bells (available at Michaels or through Amazon)

Velvet ribbon, color of your choice

If you're making the wreaths instead of buying, make a small wreath shape out of your evergreens (about 4 inches in diameter), then secure with floral wire.

If you purchased the napkin ring wreaths, well-played, you savvy shopper. Let's do this thing.

Cut a 20-inch length of the velvet ribbon for each wreath you plan to make.

Secure the ribbon to the top of the wreath for hanging it when finished. If you're not going to hang it, consider asking yourself if you ever loved the holidays, or if it's all been a big lie.

Take some velvet ribbon, place one of the bells on the ribbon and tie it to the top of the wreath so the bell hangs down in the center of the wreath.

Holding the bell, cut the ends of the ribbon to the length you desire.

Swing it around, but not like the swings at the county fair that made you nauseated in middle school. Be gentle here. This is art.

 Soundtrack tip: "Everywhere," by Fleetwood Mac (Tango in the Night, Warner, 1987). It's the opening track on Christmas Jars, *and it's got all the feels.*

HEATHER LUPO
Venice, Florida

Last year at Christmastime, a Christmas Jar appeared on my front steps. I was wondering if it had been delivered to the wrong house, but upon searching, I found that it is a tradition. It was filled with at least one hundred dollars worth of silver change, several twenties, tens, and five-dollar bills, and a few gift cards to local places.

I was overwhelmed, as it touched my heart immensely after everything we'd been through. It was the first Christmas without my husband after losing him tragically to injuries from a car accident. I vowed to keep up the tradition by delivering one myself, year after year.

This year was my first Christmas Jar that I was giving away. I have been saving my silver change all year, and filled two jars. However, since I didn't know anyone else, I'm going to save the other jar full of change for someone else next year. I just sold some items on Facebook marketplace that I no longer needed.

I took the hundred and forty dollars that I received from those, and stuffed it inside the jar with the silver change. I also had an AutoZone thirty-dollar gift card that I will not use that I put inside the jar. I didn't know who I was going to give the jar to, since I'm new here in Florida, and didn't know many people, especially ones with a hardship, or someone just needing an emotional pick me up. I had kept wondering how I would find someone in time for Christmas to give it to.

When I went to the nail salon to have my nails done last week, the nail technician was so open and sweet, and just in conversation, was telling me her story of her life here in Florida over the past couple of years. She lost her home due to a hurricane in 2004. Her husband is disabled, her car is old and in need of repair, and she works several jobs just to make ends meet. I started thinking that SHE would be the person I would want to give my jar to!

Then I came home, and after a friend was mentioning on Facebook that I needed to "armor-all" my tires on my golf cart, I went out immediately and did it. I shined them up, and took a picture to send back to him to show him that I did it. I looked closer at the tires for the first time. And, I couldn't believe it . . . the name of my tires on the golf cart happens to be the same as the nail technician's. What? I had never realized before. I took that as a sign.

I dropped the jar off for the nail tech at the salon on Saturday. I had asked someone who was walking in from the parking lot to bring it in for me so I'd remain anonymous. The next day that she worked was Tuesday. I wish I could have seen her reaction to the jar sitting on her work station. I hope that it brings her and her family some joy and peace this Christmas, as my heart is full.

Oakli's Mint Bliss Brownies

As the oldest of four siblings—and with four children of her own—Oakli has a very special set of skills. Her extensive experience swatting away smaller hands with utensils has transformed her into a renowned kitchen ninja. These talents are particularly helpful with this recipe.

Top tip: If your intended brownie recipients are already happy, consider another recipe. These brownies could cause them to exceed the recommended daily allowance of bliss.

BROWNIES

1 (18-ounce) box double chocolate brownie mix, such as Ghirardelli, or substitute

(If you prefer to make your brownies from scratch, we salute you.)

MINT FROSTING

1 cup (2 sticks) unsalted butter, softened

1 teaspoon mint extract

4 drops green food coloring

¼ cup milk

Powdered sugar, to desired consistency

CHOCOLATE FROSTING

4 tablespoons cocoa

4 tablespoons (½ stick) butter

½ cup milk or cream

Powdered sugar, to desired consistency

INSTRUCTIONS

Using the box directions and ingredients, mix and bake brownies in a 9x13 baking pan. Don't go rogue here; the stakes are too high.

MINT FROSTING INSTRUCTIONS

To make the mint frosting, mix the butter, mint extract, food coloring, and milk together. Begin adding the powdered sugar in small increments, mixing each time, to your preferred consistency for spreading. You're going to want to brush your teeth with this frosting—and honestly . . . we don't hate the idea.

CHOCOLATE FROSTING INSTRUCTIONS

To make the chocolate frosting, melt the butter in a saucepan with the cocoa.

Add ½ cup milk or cream and stir until smooth. Add the powdered sugar in small increments, mixing between additions to your preferred consistency for spreading.

To assemble, wait until the brownies have cooled, then frost with the mint frosting, covering the entire surface of the brownies. Then top with a chocolate frosting layer.

Cut, serve yourself a sample, swat away intruders, and plate the rest for friends and family.

Pairs with: Pair this with a scoop of French vanilla ice cream, such as Tillamook. Oui, oui!

Pilgrim's Pumpkin Chocolate Chip Cookies

There is no Christmas Jars movement without Pilgrim, the Wrights' beloved goldendoodle. He was present for nearly every clandestine jar delivery until his death in 2019. Pilgrim loved watching Kodi make these cookies and could often be found scavenging the floor for spots of sugar to clean up.

Top tip: Consider making these for your Thanksgiving pregame activities. They're the perfect snack for your kitchen team. Not helping with dinner? No cookies for you.

½ cup butter	1 teaspoon baking soda
1½ cups sugar	1 teaspoon baking powder
1 cup (half a 15-ounce can) pumpkin puree	1 teaspoon cinnamon
1 egg	½ teaspoon nutmeg
1 teaspoon vanilla	¼ teaspoon salt
2½ cups flour	Chocolate chips

Heat the oven to 350 degrees F. and line two cookie sheets with parchment paper.

Mix all ingredients together.

Drop full tablespoons of dough on the cookie sheets. Bake for 10–13 minutes or until the cookies are light and fluffy.

Pairs with: Pilgrim's cookies pair exceedingly well with your favorite hot chocolate, especially if you've added a dollop of whipped cream that's larger than the mug itself.

BRUCE "DUKE" BRUBAKER III
Owensboro, Kentucky

I love Christmas—the ritual, the traditions, family, and everything else that comes with the holiday. So I was super excited to hear about a book with an idea that wrapped all of those things in a bow. We did our first Christmas Jar so long ago, I can't remember the year. But I remember that first jar. The size. The decorations. The clandestine delivery. And the charity.

Fast forward to today: our boys are eighteen and twenty-one years old. They've been along for the ride on every Christmas Jar delivery, and actually made the delivery multiple times themselves.

One day we were prepping the jar for delivery, and one of the boys said, "You know, I can't remember a Christmas when we didn't deliver a Jar." How cool is that?

Each year on delivery day, I send Jason a photo of our jar and share the story. Jason has told us we're one of the original Christmas Jars pioneers and that there might not be another family that's given away more jars. What a humble honor!

The Christmas Jar tradition became part of our lives. I had no idea the impact such a simple idea would have on my family as well as the families that received a jar. We look forward to making that delivery every Christmas season.

Grandgary's Yarn Star

This yarn star is named for our grandson Gary, who, if given the chance, would hot glue himself to your living room sofa. So while this craft might be labeled as kid-friendly, we highly recommend supervision for all children, especially redheads named Gary.

Cardboard or wooden stars

Yarn in multiple colors or
multicolored yarn

Hot glue gun and glue sticks

Take a cardboard or wooden star shape and begin wrapping with yarn. If your family has a favorite college or pro sports team, use their colors for some added personalization.

Wrap in multiple directions until the entire star is covered.

Help your pint-sized assistant tuck the end of the yarn into the layers of yarn and drop a small drop of hot glue to hold it secure.

Make a yarn loop and secure it to the star.

Hang it on your tree, a rearview mirror, or a neighbor's doorknob. If your recipient also has a favorite team, discover who their rival is and make them a Grandgary's Yarn Star in the rival's colors.

 Soundtrack tip: "Christmas Star" by Debbie Gibson (Winterlicious, StarGirl, 2022).

Rancher's Lunch Bell Dream Cake

Kodi spent her formative childhood years on a ranch in Wyoming. She learned the power of family, the value of hard work, and how to admire the handsome ranch hands. Kodi fondly remembers watching them settle in for lunch and crush this cake before the dust had settled.

Top tip: This dessert makes friends faster than that one girl in fifth grade who gave away Starbursts at recess. Consider making it for large families, church Christmas dinners, or for telethon commercial breaks.

CAKE

2 cups sugar

2 cups flour

1 teaspoon baking soda

¼ teaspoon salt

2 (4-ounce) sticks butter

4 tablespoons cocoa

1 cup water

1 teaspoon vanilla extract

½ cup buttermilk (Consider making your own by adding 1 teaspoon of lemon juice or vinegar to ½ cup milk)

2 eggs

FROSTING

1 (4-ounce) stick butter

4 tablespoons cocoa

6 tablespoons buttermilk

4 cups powdered sugar

½ teaspoon vanilla extract

1 cup chopped nuts, optional

INSTRUCTIONS

Heat the oven to 350 degrees F.

Sift together sugar, flour, baking soda, and salt. Thank them for their unheralded contribution and set them aside.

Melt and stir butter and cocoa. Add 1 cup water. Bring to a rapid boil.

Pour over the dry ingredients and beat well.

Add vanilla, buttermilk, and eggs. Beat until fluffier than Grandma's feather bed.

Pour into a greased and floured 9x13 baking pan.

Bake for 30 minutes.

Turn on the oven light and take a moment or two to admire your work. But stay humble—you're not done yet; you've got frosting to make.

FROSTING INSTRUCTIONS

Heat butter, cocoa, and buttermilk in a saucepan. Remove from heat and add powdered sugar, vanilla extract, and chopped nuts. (The nuts are optional, but if you don't have an allergy to worry about, skipping the nuts could be the worst mistake of your baking life.)

Remove cake from the oven and, while still warm, place glorious globs of the frosting all over it. Let sit and melt and then spread over the cake.

Pairs with: A hearty piece of Rancher's Dream Cake pairs well with your favorite cider.

Magical Magazine Christmas Tree

Before firing up your Amazon Prime account, make a trip to your favorite thrift store for an old magazine and a used cake stand. If the employees ask what you're making, tell them to mind their own business, or they'll end up on the naughty list.

One magazine with large pages and a thin spine

Cake stand

1 (11-ounce) bottle spray adhesive, such as Elmer's

1 (10.5-ounce) bag fake snow (available at Michaels, Hobby Lobby, or through Amazon)

1 (13-ounce) bottle spray snow (available at Michaels, Hobby Lobby, or through Amazon)

Take the first page of the magazine and fold the top left corner into the spine. Fold that edge to the spine of the magazine. Fold the extra at the bottom of the page up so that the page bottom is perpendicular to the spine (the bottom of the pages will be the base of the tree).

Continue this until the entire magazine is folded. When done, it should stand on its own and—spoiler—look like a Christmas tree. If it doesn't look like a Christmas tree, squint and use your imagination.

Carry your tree outside and spray with glue and sprinkle fake snow on it, or use spray snow—whichever method you think will work best.

Place the tree on a cake stand and leave it on your neighbor's porch.

 Soundtrack tip: "Christmas Tree Farm" by Taylor Swift (Christmas Tree Farm [EP], Republic, 2019).

Real Men Wear Kilts Scotcheroos

If you're even considering making these without wearing a kilt, or at least printing off photos of men in kilts and taping them to the refrigerator, why are you even in the kitchen? Fun fact: These scotcheroos are the official cookie of Scotland. (Please don't Google that. Just trust your authors.)

Top tip: Try making these with a friend and insist you both use thick Scottish accents. If one of you slips, you must sing the Scottish national anthem. (Also with an accent.)

1¼ cups honey

¾ cup light brown sugar

1¼ cups creamy peanut butter

1 teaspoon vanilla extract

6 cups puffed rice cereal, such as Rice Krispies

Nonstick cooking spray

1½ cups semisweet chocolate chips

1½ cups butterscotch chips

1 tablespoon coconut oil

In a medium saucepan, heat the honey and brown sugar over medium heat, stirring frequently, until the sugar is dissolved, 5 to 7 minutes. Do. Not. Boil. The results can be catastrophic.

Remove the mixture from the heat and stir in the peanut butter and vanilla. As you stir, ask yourself this deep question: Why aren't peanut butter and vanilla used together more frequently? And who's to blame?

Put the cereal in a large bowl, pour the peanut butter mixture over it, and stir until well coated.

Spray the cooking spray of your choice onto a 9x13 baking pan. Press the cereal mixture evenly into the prepared pan.

In a microwave-safe bowl, combine the chocolate chips, butterscotch chips, and coconut oil. Search for 3 to 5 butterscotch chips that didn't get hit with the oil and carefully remove them. Eat.

Microwave the mixture at 50 percent power in 15-second intervals until the chocolate is melted. If this takes more than two minutes, order a new microwave on Amazon.

Stir the mixture until well combined and fully melted.

Pour the mixture over the cereal, spreading it until even. Refrigerate the bars until firm, at least 30 minutes.

 Soundtrack tip: "Auld Lang Syne" by Rod Stewart (Merry Christmas, Baby, Universal, 2012).

Rudolph's Maple Carrot Cupcakes

You might think Rudolph's greatest contribution to Christmas is his nose, and while we certainly honor his noble nostrils, the Wrights also cherish his Maple Carrot Cupcakes. And it's time you do too. Please note that this recipe has a higher degree of difficulty than others in this collection, but what else would you expect from a reindeer who leads a team on a global adventure on a single night?

Top tip: Rudolph has watched you with some of these other recipes, and he has concerns. Why pull out all the ingredients before you need them? Your counter looks like a baker's estate sale. Try pulling out the ingredients as you need them. Do it for Rudolph.

CUPCAKES

2 cups all-purpose flour

1 cup sugar

1 teaspoon baking powder

1 teaspoon baking soda

1 teaspoon cinnamon

½ teaspoon salt

4 large eggs, room temperature

1 cup olive oil

½ cup maple syrup

3 cups carrots, grated
  (about 6 medium carrots)

Paper baking cups

FROSTING

1 (8-ounce) package cream cheese,
  softened

¼ cup butter, softened

¼ cup maple syrup

1 teaspoon vanilla extract

INSTRUCTIONS

Heat the oven to 350 degrees F. Prepare two muffin tins with paper baking cups (18 in all). In a large bowl, combine the flour, sugar, baking powder, baking soda, cinnamon, and salt.

In another bowl, beat eggs, oil, and syrup. Don't get cute and use the same bowl. Trust the process.

Slowly stir wet ingredients into dry ingredients until moistened. Fold in carrots.

Fill 18 prepared muffin cups two-thirds full.

Bake for 20–25 minutes, but also rely on the scientifically tested method used since the dawn of time. Insert a toothpick into the center and if it comes out clean, the cupcakes are donezo.

Cool for 5 minutes before removing from pans to wire racks.

FROSTING INSTRUCTIONS

For frosting, combine all ingredients in a bowl and beat until smooth.

Frost when cupcakes are cool, then store them in the refrigerator.

Pairs with: These cupcakes pair perfectly with a piece of paper and a pen. While savoring one, write two letters. One to Santa, obviously, and one to Rudolph thanking him for his recipe and his leadership in our turbulent world.

WRIGHT FAMILY MEMORY
Kason Wright

For me, there was definitely one Christmas Jar experience that was the most memorable. A family was suggested to us that might need a little boost. We didn't know them very well; we felt like this family was the right fit. We had a hard time finding the house at first because our GPS tried to send us to some neighborhood in Australia. So after a few phone calls, we got the right address and were happy to see that we would not be getting on a plane to deliver our Christmas Jar.

Everyone but the driver walked up the stairs, and we quickly determined an escape route before setting the jar down and knocking. We all ran off, but for some reason ended up going in different directions. That meant that I ended up alone on the other side of the building. I heard them open the door, and someone leaned over the balcony, yelling, "I think I see someone!"

I put up my hood and tried to blend in, casually walking in the direction the rest of the family had gone. The weather had been bad, and there was a lot of mud. Because of that, the car had gotten stuck so it took longer for them to circle back than I expected, plus our dog, Pilgrim, was barking like crazy from inside the car. So I found a power line pole and tried to stay hidden behind it as best I could until the car came around.I hopped in, and I may or may not have yelled, "Well, I am not doing *that* ever again!" Then I gave a very detailed play-by-play. Even though it was cold and stressful because I thought for sure I got caught, it was worth it all—and as it turned out, I definitely did it again the next year, and every year since.

GLUTEN
FREE

Santa's Strawberry Jam

Santa's a busy guy, but if he ever added a modern kitchen to his North Pole Operations Center, this jam would be among its first offerings. When Mrs. Claus is under the weather, he makes her this strawberry jam. When one of his elves hits the mandatory retirement age of 299, Santa gives the elf some jam. And when the firm hits their toy quotas and Christmas goes off without a hitch, everyone on the management team gets a jar.

Top tip: When you're making this particular Christmas gift, someone is going to come into the kitchen and say, "Oh! I've heard Santa loves that stuff. It's his jam." Don't laugh at this—it only encourages them.

1 (16-ounce) container fresh strawberries

1¼ cups granulated sugar

1-2 tablespoons fresh-squeezed lemon juice

Use jars large enough to hold up to two cups of jam. Sterilize them in boiling water and dry completely. Set aside.

Remove the strawberry tops and dice up the berries. If still in the room, the same person who made the "It's his jam" joke might take one of the berry stem tops and put it on his chin like a soul patch. That one's decent; you can laugh at that.

Place strawberries, sugar, and lemon juice in a deep saucepan.

Stir to coat the strawberries.

Let strawberries sit for 10–15 minutes until they release their juices. And, if applicable, the kraken.

Turn the heat to medium low and stir with a rubber spatula until the sugar has melted completely.

Be sure to scrape any sugar off the sides of the pot and the spatula. All sugar must be dissolved to prevent the finished jam from crystallizing.

Simmer for 10–15 minutes while stirring frequently and mashing the strawberries with a potato masher or something similar as they soften.

Bring mixture to a full rolling boil. Boil until the mixture reaches 220 degrees F. Stir constantly to keep the mixture from burning.

Remove from heat. Pour into prepared jars, leaving at least ¼ inch space at the top.

Place the jar lid on immediately and allow it to cool at room temperature.

Refrigerate until firm and write Santa a letter detailing your experiences. He loves the feedback.

Packaging tip: This is a perfect opportunity to introduce your jam recipient to the Christmas Jars tradition. Consider including a note with your gift that explains the tradition and invites them to use the jar to collect money when the jam is gone.

Not for Adults Gift Tags

Listen, you have your own gift tags, those fancy things you make or buy that look like they came from the Regency Era. These are *not* those. Our "Not for Adults Gift Tags" are intended to be made *by* kids and *for* kids. All other use is prohibited by law.

Premade kraft or cardstock paper gift tags (not from the Regency Era)

Crayons

Paint

Rubber stamps and stamp ink

Announce to all the people in your home, neighborhood, or zip code that it's craft day.

Arrange the supplies on a table and give your crafters an inspiring speech. Pull a few lines from *Gladiator*, *Independence Day*, or *Troll 2*. Be sure they know this is as close to a no-rules crafting experience as they're likely to have before they're legal adults. Set them loose to make all the gift tags they'll need.

As your crew works, choose one of the simple recipes from this book for a crafting snack—sharing optional, but encouraged. After all, you're going to be using some of the gift tags they're making.

Packaging tip: Can there really be a packaging tip for a packaging craft? Naturally! If you have an especially productive tag maker, take 8 to 10 tags and put them in a small cellophane gift bag. Then add a—wait for it—gift tag to the bag and give it to someone with a long Christmas list.

Not That Kind of Wallflower Pinecone Hanging

Don't be shy—tackle this more challenging craft and trust that your friends and neighbors will be showing off this gift for a long time. Some handmade gifts barely make it to Christmas, but this one is likely to last until both you and Santa retire.

SUPPLIES

3x3 unfinished wooden squares (available at Michaels, Walmart, or through Amazon)

Acrylic craft paint in complementary colors

Glue sticks

Decorative moss

Pinecones collected from outdoors or from Michaels, Hobby Lobby, or Amazon

Velvet ribbon

TOOLS

Paintbrushes (small and large artist brushes and a small foam brush)

Hot glue gun

You can either choose to leave the panels natural or paint them black using the foam brush. But decide now, or you'll face an afternoon of regret.

Cut your large pinecones in 1½- to 2-inch thicknesses to create the flowers.

Cut the tops off of the medium-size pinecones to create smaller flowers.

For any smaller pinecones you find, leave them as they are and don't tease them.

Set aside any pieces of the pinecones that may have fallen off. You can use these as leaves.

To paint your pinecone flowers, choose colors that go together like a bouquet. Imagine you're planning your sister's wedding again, but this time it's actually under budget.

Paint each pinecone scale on top, leaving the center unpainted.

To paint the center, choose a yellow or cream, dabbing it on so that the points from the pinecone give it dimension.

If you choose, you can take some pieces of the pinecone scales and paint them green to use as leaves around the flower.

If you have some mini or skinny pinecones, paint the entire cone. Gently swipe your brush up the pinecone, leaving some of the texture and dimension of the pinecone to show through.

After your pinecones are all painted, lay out some moss on the panel as a background. Hot glue the moss to the panel.

Lay out your pinecone flowers in any design you enjoy and hot glue them on. If you chose to paint leaves, place them around the flowers and hot glue them down. Consider asking yourself and your crafting partners how the world functioned before hot glue guns.

To complete the panel so that it can hang on the wall, cut an 8-inch piece of ribbon and hot glue one end to the back side of the top left corner and the other end to the back side of the top right corner.

Packaging tip: Instead of wrapping or placing this delicate creation in a gift bag, consider handing it to your recipient or carefully hanging it on their doorknob.

ANONYMOUS
Franklin, North Carolina

Ever since I was a recipient of a Christmas Jar in 2021, I've wanted to spread the joy and hope that it brought me. I started my first Christmas Jar in 2023. I was a single mom on food stamps and money was tight, but I was determined to still do a Christmas Jar and give what I could. Giving that first Jar anonymously felt amazing.

I just gave my second one this year and was able to be even more generous with its contents than I was the first time. It brings me such joy and excitement to put my loose change and several bills in that Jar throughout the whole year. Even now, when my young son finds coins on the ground he now wants to put them in our Christmas Jar.

I love the consistent opportunity during the year to turn outwards and see how I can serve and bless others and be looking for the one needing that extra boost. This is something I plan to do every year for as long as I live.

I'd prefer to remain anonymous because I live in a small rural town.

Sift and Gift Hot Chocolate Mix

This tried-and-true classic presents another ideal opportunity to spread the Christmas Jar giving tradition. You don't know it yet, but the jar you're about to fill with this heavenly mix and then give away could eventually change someone's life. Yep, you're pretty great, no matter what Brock said about you in ninth-grade gym class.

Top tip: Consider making a larger batch of mix for multiple jars. Why make just one? More jars + more hot chocolate = more joy. It's just math.

2 cups powdered sugar

1 cup unsweetened cocoa powder

2 cups powdered milk or instant nonfat dry milk

Sift the powdered sugar and the cocoa powder into a large bowl. If you've doubled or tripled the recipe, which we highly recommend, the sifting is even more important. Nothing ruins hot chocolate quite like lumps, and you don't want to be giving that away at Christmas. Well, unless the gift is for Brock, then let him have his lumps.

Stir in the powdered milk and whisk well until perfectly combined.

Pour into a jar and add mini marshmallows to the top.

Packaging tip: Write "Christmas Jar" on the lid or side of the jar. When gifting, explain how the jar can be repurposed to bless someone else next year.

The Less Famous Reindeer Pops

Few readers will know that these scrumptious pops are one of the reasons Rudolph felt so ostracized by his peers. They didn't just shut him out of the reindeer games; they ate these desserts while Rudolph watched from across the field. So when it came time to include this recipe in our book, Rudolph agreed, but only with the "less famous" name adjustment. Reindeer are so silly sometimes.

Top tip: Gather the littles! These are very kid- and adult-but-think-like-a-kid-friendly. You know who you are.

1 (25-ounce) package chocolate sandwich cookies, such as Double Stuf Oreos, or substitute

Wooden craft sticks

2 (10-ounce) bags chocolate melting wafers, such as Ghirardelli, or substitute

Waxed paper

Red candy-coated chocolate candies, such as M&M's (or cinnamon Imperials, such as Brach's)

Candy eyeballs (available through Amazon)

1 (16-ounce) bag mini pretzels, such as Rold Gold Tiny Twists (broken in ½-inch pieces)

Gently stick a craft stick into the white filling of a Double Stuf Oreo. Repeat this for as many reindeer pops as you want to make. If you're not making enough for everyone in your life who loves Christmas, take a seat and do some self-reflection.

Melt the chocolate and coat each pop well. Place each one on a cookie sheet lined with waxed paper.

After you dip each pop and before the chocolate sets up, attach 4 pieces of the pretzels to the top. These are antlers and they're exactly to scale.

Add two eyes. If you want to annoy the rest of the pops, add a red candy nose so they all dress like Rudolph for the day.

 Soundtrack tip: "Grandma Got Run Over by a Reindeer" by Elmo & Patsy (Grandma Got Run Over by a Reindeer, *Sony Legacy, 1988).*

Sandi's Macrame Christmas Tree Picture

Have you met Jason's mother? Not yet? You really should. She's the kind of mother, grandmother, and great-grandmother everyone should know. And Sandi loves a well-made macrame craft. In fact, she has a craft cabin in her yard with more macrame than your local artisans festival.

Picture frame (thrift store anyone?)

Burlap fabric (just enough to cover the backing of the frame)

Hot glue gun and glue sticks

4 (6-inch) lengths 3–5 mm macrame cord (color of your choice; available at Michaels, Hobby Lobby, or through Amazon)

3 (6-inch) lengths gold embroidery floss, such as DMC E3852 or DMC E3821 (available at Michaels, Hobby Lobby, or through Amazon)

11 (10-inch) lengths gold embroidery floss (same as above, just different lengths)

1 (4- to 6-inch) straight-ish branch (or dowel if you don't want this to be *too* rustic)

Comb

Hair spray

Small wooden star or length of grosgrain ribbon

Scissors

First take apart the frame and discard the artwork inside and remove the glass. If you don't like the color of your frame, grab some spray paint in the color you like and spray your frame. If the artwork you inherited from the thrift store looks valuable, do a reverse image search and consider selling on eBay.

Grab your burlap and cut out enough to cover the hard back from the picture frame.

Lay the burlap over the hard backing and carefully place a thin line of hot glue down the right edge of the backing. Attach your burlap to that line of glue.

Hold it down until it falls in love and sticks.

Continued on page 110

Continued from page 108

Place another thin line of glue along the bottom, attaching the burlap while pulling it tighter than you might have thought possible just minutes ago.

Repeat the same action along the top.

Once the three sides are secure, glue down the left side with a thin line of glue.

You want to be careful about the amount of glue you use, as it can very easily seep through the burlap and show on the front. Plus it will stick to your fingers, and you'll be gnawing it off until Groundhog Day.

Cut off any excess burlap around the edges and set it aside.

TREE INSTRUCTIONS

Take your 6-inch lengths of macrame cord and unravel them into three separate pieces (you will be using 11 pieces of 6-inch macrame cord).

Do the same to your three 6-inch pieces of gold embroidery floss. (You should end up with 18 pieces of 6-inch embroidery floss). Set them to the side, but not so far that they feel abandoned. These will be used to tie around the macrame and gold thread tassels.

Take one of your 10-inch gold threads and break it apart into four smaller threads. Take one of the 6-inch pieces of macrame rope and fold it in half. Working individually, fold the four smaller threads in half, then take two of them and place them on the back side of the folded macrame cord. Take the other two gold threads and place them on the front of the folded macrame. If you don't have to reread those last few sentences, you might be a member of Mensa.

At the top of the folded threads and cord, tie one of the 6-inch pieces of gold thread around the top, creating a small loop, kind of like a little head on a creepy elf doll.

Tie the 6-inch cord in a square knot and place a small dot of hot glue at the knot to secure it. Carefully use your comb to comb out the macrame cord and gold threads so that it makes a fluffy tassel.

Repeat that same process for the other 10 pieces—you'll have 11 tassels when done.

Next, trim the bottom of the tassels individually so they're even. Start by laying out all your tassels from shortest to longest in length. Once you have the shortest one, cut it off even at the bottom, being careful not to cut too much off. Measure each remaining tassel to that first one, so they're all the same length. Measure twice, cut once. Send your high school shop teacher a text. He or she was right!

Assemble your frame, putting the back with the burlap back into the frame opening.

Cut your branch to make the trunk of the tree. Hot glue the branch to the burlap in the center of the frame, with the bottom edge touching the bottom of the frame.

Lay your tassels out on the frame before hot-gluing them down, starting with five on the bottom with the tops of the tassels touching and angled out at the bottom to make the first tier of tree boughs. The next row will have three tassels. Lay them out the same way, creating another tier of boughs. The next row will have two tassels, and the final layer will be one tassel in the center.

After you've laid it out and like how it looks, take the top layers of tassels off and begin hot-gluing them back in place to create your tree. Carefully comb out your tassels so that they lay out nicely.

Cut off any of the gold threads that won't lie down. If they won't, threaten them with extra Saturday chores.

On the top of the tree, glue either a wooden star or a velvet ribbon bow.

Delivery tip: Can you imagine sneaking this nifty gifty onto your neighbor's mantel when they're not noticing? Add the most ridiculous photo of your family for added effect.

SISKA AND DAVID WOODSON
Strasburg, Virginia

We moved to Strasburg, Virginia, from the Fairfax, Virginia, area in 2017. We both grew up in the city, but my husband was living in Strasburg for a brief time before he met me, and he always told me he has a special feeling for the town. My husband, David Woodson, was a diesel mechanic in Vienna, Virginia, and during COVID he would go in to work every day, because his job was considered essential. April 20, 2020, is when everything changed for us. I received a phone call that he had been in a car accident—a bad one, I was told. The first thing in my mind was that he was gone. But God spared his life. However, he became completely paralyzed. Because this was at the height of COVID, I can't even begin to tell you how hard it was that I had to watch him struggle alone in the hospital for several weeks and then for weeks at Shepherd Center, the rehab hospital in Atlanta, as well. Many of our friends and family—and myself—fought really hard to get me in with him at Shepherd Center.

Moving forward in time, we had to sell our home, look for another one, and make a lot of changes in our lives to accommodate his disability needs. From him losing jobs, his insurance, and his retirement over this time was financially challenging. The police declared it a no-fault accident, because there was no proof how the accident happened. The person who cut him off that morning walked out with only bruises and had no full-coverage insurance. So this was hard to deal with, not only on the financial aspect, but also emotionally and physically for the both of us. Especially for Dave when he was told by the doctor that his chances to walk were slim to none and that the possibility of being independent was slim to none as well.

Fast-forward four and a half years later—where we are today. We have so many testimonies of God's grace and kindness to us through people around us, but this will take hours to tell. To make it short, God is always good, He always prevails, and He works in such mysterious ways that at the end you will find yourself wondering how it happened. How did it work out perfectly? That does not make sense to me, but it makes sense to Him, and His plan and outcome is always more perfect than what you would have thought.

The Christmas Jar came to us about three and a half years ago. We had just found the house we are living in now; it was just completed in the beginning of 2021, and we moved to the new house then. We were still figuring things out, finding our new normal. Also, Strasburg has been one of our biggest supporters. The community and the friends we made here are truly God-sent.

Since we were rejected from getting any medical assistance from the government, all of David's caregiving, medical supplies, transport, etc., needed to be paid out of pocket, so the funds really helped us. However, that fund quickly ran out and the next thing we knew, we were trying to figure out how to pay caregiving costs along with the holidays approaching.

When I mentioned how God works in mysterious ways—I don't remember exactly the day, but I was busy trying to get Dave to bed, and I heard a doorbell.

I opened my door, but no one was there. But what I saw was your book and the mason jar with money and coins. I was struck with overwhelming emotion. Dave and I counted, and it had about $250 in that jar—that was just enough to pay the caregiver for that week. We both were just so touched and so grateful. The person remained anonymous but had left us a very touching note. I unfortunately can't locate that note anymore, since at the time things were still a mess from the move. But your book gave us hope and comfort that there are still many good, loving, and kind people in this changing world. Moving forward to this day, Dave has been getting some stronger upper movement. He is still paralyzed, but he is now gaining some independence back. He is able to drive and eat by himself. Him being appointed to the town council gave him hope and a sense of purpose in life. The Christmas Jar has taught us to continue to fight, be kind, be loving to others no matter what hard challenges you have, and to pay this kindness forward, because no matter what there are many others out there who are struggling, and everyone could use help once in a while.

For the next two years since we received that Christmas Jar, I have been wondering who gave it to us, but mostly wanted to get to know the person who came up with this kind and loving idea. But then the idea kind of went away, because I said to myself, maybe it's not meant for us to know who gave to us rather than seeing it as God's blessing, so I stopped wondering. Then, that night at the county's dinner when I read the program and saw your name, and the book title *Christmas Jars*, I immediately knew who you were and felt so grateful that Dave and I have been blessed by this mission. I could not stop getting emotional when you started speaking, and as I am writing this as well. The emotion is still there years later, because this has impacted our lives.

We intend to keep the Christmas Jar going this year. We have not used the jar in a few years; we just have been paying it forward in other ways. But this year, we will do it. God is reminding us that we need to keep the Christmas Jar mission going.

Shane's Star Anise Wreath

Named for one of our grandkiddos, this wreath is guaranteed to make you smile just like Shane. Wide, toothy, and with a dash of mischievousness. And while we encourage caution anytime wire and a hot glue gun are involved, we have faith that with supervision, the youngins in your life can contribute to this particular project.

14- or 16-gauge floral or hobby wire (available at Michaels, Hobby Lobby, or through Amazon)

2 (3.5-ounce) packages star anise (available through Walmart.com or Amazon)

Hot glue gun and glue sticks

Ribbon

Lay out your star anise in a circle as large as you want your wreath to be. If you're not sure what a star anise is, ask Siri. This wreath looks better if there are two layers, so count out enough star anise for the second layer.

Make a wire circle the same size as your star anise circle. You'll make the wire circle several layers so that it's strong enough to hold its shape.

Hold the hot glue gun, but let your mini-me pull the trigger. Have that child yell, "Glue stick 'em up!" They won't get it, but you'll giggle.

Hot glue the star anise against the wire circle, then add a second layer overlapping the first.

Use ribbon to make a loop and a bow for hanging. Tell your helper he or she did a great job, even if they have glue in their hair.

Delivery tip: Like some of the other crafts we've presented, this one requires some care with delivery. Rather than wrapping, consider handing it to your recipient and explaining the process. If they offer to make one for you in return, tell them you have a child who'd love to help.

Wooden Friendship Ring Ornaments

The Wrights can humbly witness that these popular ornaments are proven to deepen friendships with even the grumpiest of grinches. These are especially effective gifts for coworkers, church friends, and vloggers.

1 package (2- to 3-inch) natural wooden rings (available at Michaels, Hobby Lobby, or through Amazon); you will use six for this craft (but you can use others for Grandma Sarah's Wooden Ring Garland on page 64)

Black acrylic paint

1 package round chalkboard tags (available at Michaels, Hobby Lobby, dollar stores, or through Amazon)

Acrylic paint pens

Hot glue and glue sticks

Paintbrushes

Ribbon of your choosing

Paint the rings black. When dry, lay a ring on a chalkboard tag and trace it. Do this for all six ornaments.

Cut out the circle from the chalkboard tag. Try not to imagine the sound of nails on a chalkboard. That's a surefire holiday buzzkill.

With the acrylic paint pens, create whatever image you want for your ornament, making sure to set the ring on top from time to time to make sure your image fits within the ring.

Once painted, cut a couple of millimeters from around the edge of the tag.

Place hot glue around the edge of the tag and carefully place a painted ring on it.

Measure and cut your ribbon into 7-inch strips and hot glue one to the back of each ornament at the top, creating a loop so it can be hung on a tree—or your grandfather's ear when he's sleeping in his recliner.

As a final touch, decorate the top of the ornament with embellishments of your choice.

 Soundtrack tip: How the Grinch Stole Christmas—*full album (Mercury/ Polygram, 1995).*

Zucchini Joy Bread

This bread can't bring about world peace, guarantee you a promotion, or heal the rift between you and your brother-in-law Byron over "the incident" at the reunion. But it will bring your recipients joy. It's in the name, and the Wrights wouldn't lead you astray. Byron, maybe, but not you.

3 eggs	1 teaspoon salt
2 cups sugar	1 teaspoon baking soda
1 cup olive oil	¼ teaspoon baking powder
1 teaspoon vanilla extract	2 cups grated zucchini
1 teaspoon cinnamon	3 cups flour

Heat the oven to 350 degrees F., and if your kitchen already smells like something else, crack a window or door to cleanse the kitchen air palate.

Beat eggs until foamy.

Add sugar, oil, vanilla, cinnamon, salt, baking soda, baking powder, zucchini, and flour. As you mix well, think only happy thoughts. It matters.

Turn the batter into a greased and floured loaf pan and bake for 1 hour and 20 minutes. Oven times vary, and with longer baking times it's always wise to stay close in those final moments.

Remove from the pan, place on the cooling rack, and ask yourself if you're feeling more joyful than when you started. If not, eat this loaf and make another batch for your friends and neighbors.

 Soundtrack tip: "The First Noel" by Jenny Oaks Baker & Family Four (Joy to the World, 2020).

GLENDA RAY DUNNING
Sarasota, Florida

My jar is almost full. It is my first jar, and it is on the counter by a very happy accident. A couple months ago, I was scanning a bookseller's listings for something to add to my annual Christmas reading list, and I saw your book. I read the excerpt and knew it would be perfect. As I cried my way through the book, I knew it will be one that I will read every year. As I said, I have not yet given my first jar. I have passed on the book to two dozen of the people I work with at my charities, people who I know will by now have jars on their counters and have passed the message to friends who will eagerly make this a part of their lives.

The only problem will be to decide who to give my jar to. So many in my community are still suffering from our recent hurricanes. While it is considered a wealthy community, there are still many who have to make difficult decisions every day. Do I buy groceries or my medications? Do I pay my health insurance, or do I buy homeowners insurance? I have heard of dozens who have had to make those decisions this year, and many who now have no home. And many for whom my jar would simply let them know they are not completely alone in the world and that someone cares.

Every day when I put my change in my jar, and when I read your book, I am taken back to my great-grandmother's kitchen. She was a devout woman who could barely keep the lights on but took in her two granddaughters. In the late summer, that kitchen was a whirl of the vegetables she grew in every inch of her yard, with bubbling pots of everything she could put in a jar. I was barely past being a toddler but could count to ten, so as the jars cooled and popped, it was my job to count them and put every tenth jar on the long table on the porch. There, my mom would carefully place them in boxes with cardboard between them and Daddy would load the boxes into our station wagon and drive off with them.

It wasn't until I was about seven or eight that I learned about tithing. It also took me back to the stories of my daddy's grandfather who owned large swathes of land in Missouri and Arkansas who refused to allow the stores to become company stores. During the Depression he would send his brother to Florida every December so that every child of every employee would have an orange for Christmas and candy (which he bought by the bushel basket), and I heard from so many of his elderly employees that he even made certain that all had medical attention and an acre of land that they could plant with vegetables and sell the excess as they saw fit. He established the foundation I now manage. I am fortunate that I grew up knowing that it is my duty to help where I can. I am asked often why I do not just attend the events of the charities with which I am involved and I can only answer that nothing compares to the tired I feel after arriving at 5:00 a.m. to help set up, work the event, and finally get to bed at 2:00 the next morning after helping break down.

Thank you for writing such a wonderful reminder of our responsibility to those around us. I worry that it is lost on many today, but your book brings it back. What a happy accident for me.

CHRISTMAS JARS

JOURNEY

TRAILS TO A TRADITION

JASON F. WRIGHT

Since 2005, the simple act of collecting spare change in a jar and anonymously giving it away during the holidays has brought the true spirit of Christmas to thousands of people nationwide.

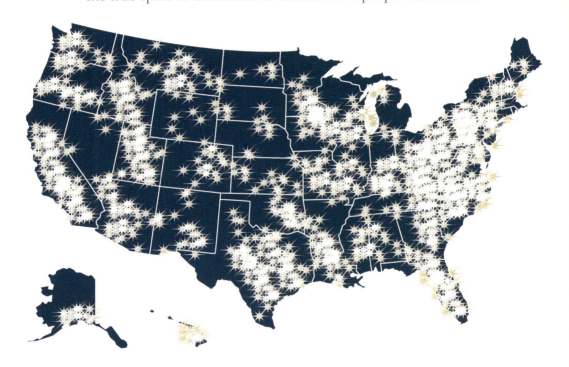

Communities where jar sightings have been reported to christmasjars.com

2005

I'm sitting at my computer in the early morning hours of December 26, 2005. We're living in a shoebox home in Fairfax, Virginia, and my two daughters and baby boy are tucked away in happy slumber.

My wife, Kodi, is sleeping, too. The rest is well deserved; the holidays have taken a toll.

Earlier that year, I'd been laid off from a small, public policy nonprofit, and I was trying to make it on my own as a consultant and political writer.

I'd also decided to pen a novella based on an experiment my family attempted during the previous Christmas season. We'd created a concept that didn't even have a name yet. It was simply a jar of change on the counter that was to be given away during the holidays.

It hadn't started as a Christmas Jar, but it had evolved into exactly that.

My book by the same name had come out in September of 2005 and by every stretch exceeded our expectations. Perhaps most unexpected was my first of many appearances on the Glenn Beck radio and television shows. His enthusiastic embrace of the book took it from a regional hit to a book selling out across the country.

The sweetness of that Christmas night lingers like the smell of fresh pie, and I sit at my iMac and read a few book reviews that have popped up online during the day. It's an opportunity for me to enjoy the final moments of Christmas before life wakes up on December 26.

With the ding of a digital bell, an email lands in my inbox. I don't recognize the sender, and because it seems ninety percent of my mail is trash, I nearly delete it.

"No, thanks," I whisper to my screen. "I've already got that Nigerian prince wiring me a couple million any day now."

Still, something nudges me to open it. I have absolutely no idea that the email will change my life in ways I will not understand for years.

It's appropriate, perhaps, because the story of the Christmas Jar really began a couple of decades earlier.

The Giving Gene

Growing up, service was wired into my family's DNA. My parents were exceptionally service-oriented, and, as the youngest of four children, I observed my parents inspiring my siblings to live the same way.

Sometimes the service was well-organized, a permanent fixture on the calendar. The blood drives, the annual Apple Dumpling Sales at the Community Charity Fair, cleaning the arena after University of Virginia basketball games.

Other times, it was spontaneous. Giving a ride to a stranger on the side of the road who was headed in the opposite direction from our destination. Letting people stay in our home, befriending the lonely, or adopting families for Christmas.

For my dad, it was opening doors for women and putting the needs of everyone else ahead of his own. He was that larger-than-life Tommy Lee Jones figure from *The Fugitive.* "What I want from each and every one of you is a hard-target search of every gas station, residence, warehouse, farmhouse, henhouse, outhouse, and doghouse in that area."

Then he would take a long breath. "And when you find them, serve them."

Dad's desire to serve wasn't restricted to those cases, either. He also found himself in a few key situations to perform the kind of heroic service that saves lives.

We once encountered two people fighting in their parked car in the middle of the road. As I watched from the back seat, my dad climbed right into their car. I can still see him sitting between them in the front seat, mediating peace.

When a next-door neighbor was the victim of a brutal stabbing, Dad literally held the bleeding woman together in his arms until emergency personnel arrived. Because of him, she lived.

He also invested countless hours during the holidays creating the most unusual gifts for those who needed a little bit of light and love.

He might be embarrassed by the term, but I call this desire to serve "The Giving Gene."

He had it.

My siblings and my mother also had it.

I didn't. Unlike premature graying, evidently this gene is choosey.

I simply wasn't interested in devoting that kind of time to other people. I had too many other things to worry about.

You know, really important things, *like myself.*

In 1987, just before Christmas, my father passed away on an otherwise uneventful Friday night. Even before the grass fought its way through the dirt covering his picturesque countryside grave, I began to realize I'd missed a tremendous opportunity to learn from him.

God had blessed me with the great gift of a service mentor, but I'd never really opened up the package.

Dealing with his loss at my young age was tough enough, but on top of that, I was convinced he'd died disappointed that I hadn't progressed further during our time together. So I simply operated on faith that at some point the Giving Gene would somehow activate.

Maybe I'd hit a service growth spurt?

To keep myself busy, and because some terrific teachers recommended it, I began to write more than ever over the next two years. I wrote plays, short stories, and poetry and began finding my voice as a storyteller.

(Disclaimer: The poetry was awful, and the plays were about bunny rabbits who wore leather jackets, rode motorcycles, and solved crime. But I held a single helping of hope that putting pen to paper—or fingers to a keyboard—would be good for my soul.)

In 1993, I married my best friend, Kodi, and we eventually made our way from Utah back to Virginia for that job in politics and public policy. For the first time in my life, I was being paid to write.

While I wasn't exactly telling the most compelling stories, I was writing and speaking about issues that were important to me—education, freedom, and families.

It was the beginning of something. I just didn't know what.

A Jar Is Born

In October 2004, I noticed something stirring within me. I felt the clock ticking on my opportunity to become better friends with my father's legacy. I thought often of his love of the holidays and how I couldn't remember a single year that had ever been about *him*.

They were always about *Him*.

By then, Kodi and I had two young daughters and a baby boy, and I longed to be *that* kind of father.

My father understood what it meant to celebrate Christmas every day by celebrating the Savior every day. Christmas shouldn't be a one-day holiday circled on the calendar like an appointment with the dentist, an appliance repair man, or God.

Christmas can be a way of life.

During this memorable month, I considered a long list of ideas that might prompt and inspire me to better follow my father's example.

I brainstormed how I could do good for others every day in ways that neither of us might recognize immediately. I imagined an accumulation of goodwill, like an investment that slowly grows.

When viewed as separate pieces of the puzzle, they'd be rather ordinary. But when connected, they'd create a significant season of service.

Late one October evening, I felt especially blue. The holidays were approaching again, and Kodi and I discussed our frustration that none of the traditions we'd experimented with in years past had really stuck.

Was there something we could do to help break the cycle?

Was there a new tradition we could launch in our home to help the family—mostly me—better appreciate the concept of perpetual service?

We sought something that would encourage us to think of others every single day, even if they were strangers to us.

We wanted a moment of small but sacred sacrifice, just a few seconds that reminded us of the meaning of Christmas and to keep our eyes open to the needs of others.

By the time we said good night, an idea was born. We decided to place an empty pickle jar on the counter and commit all our spare change to it each night.

We pinky-promised to drop our quarters, dimes, nickels, and pennies in the jar and to think of our brothers and sisters. It was just a slice of service and a simple gesture, and we wondered who we could bless with our modest gift.

Everyone would participate. We invited our girls to search for change and drop it in the jar. As the weeks passed, they learned to save the change from ice cream day at school, to plunge their little hands into the couch cushions, and to keep an eye on the cup holders in the family cars.

There was something special about the way the first coins sounded when they danced against the bottom of the glass jar. It was the greatest Christmas soundtrack I'd ever heard.

Over the next eight weeks, the jar grew slowly, like a good idea. When Kodi went to the dry cleaners and paid with cash, all the change went in the jar. If the children bought a treat at 7-Eleven, they paid with cash and, even if what remained was just a few pennies, they dumped their change into the jar.

The closer we got to Christmas, the more often we paid in cash when a credit card would have been more convenient. We resisted the urge to use coins to make exact change and used another bill instead to maximize the change that would find its way into the jar.

When Christmas Eve arrived, there might not have been a coin to be found within five miles of our house—except in the jar. When we counted the coins, we were surprised to see that our efforts had accumulated to just over eighty-eight dollars in mostly nickels, dimes, and pennies.

Then came the question: Now what?

We could have easily taken the money to the bank and donated by cash or check to our church or favorite charity. We might have swept it in one swift motion into a Salvation Army bucket in a bustling parking lot.

Not this year, we thought. We felt a drive to bless someone unexpectedly, someone who might not be on anyone's holiday assistance radar.

Most importantly, we wanted to do it anonymously

We made a long list of people who might benefit from the money. We knew what we had wasn't enough money to change anyone's life, but to the right person in the right situation, it could be a blessing. We considered teachers, neighbors, and coworkers, past and present. We even imagined giving it to a stranger in a parking lot.

Our discussions circled and landed on a specific family we knew and loved. They had a young man about to leave on a volunteer mission for his church, and while the family was by no means poor, we knew that it had been expensive to get the young man out the door. The mission experience would cost the young man and his family more than $10,000.

Would our meager gift sustain him or get him over the hump? Certainly not. But it would send a message that we were aware of his family and felt gratitude for both our friendship and his desire to serve God.

The next few hours of Christmas Eve 2004 played out like a scene from a Christmas movie. And not the one you just watch once, but the kind you watch every year, even after you've memorized the dialogue.

Picture this:

My wife drove, and I rode shotgun in our stealthy, silver minivan. My two daughters, ages eight and five, were excited for the adventure. Our one-year-old baby boy was just along for the ride. His turn to join the Christmas Jars delivery team would come down the road.

We rolled through the neighborhoods until we arrived at the target house a few miles away. I felt like Tom Cruise in *Mission Impossible*. I only lacked the spy skills, music, and ability to do my own stunts.

At least I had the lovely leading lady!

When my wife parked the minivan and let us out, my daughters were suddenly uninterested in the adventure. It took some convincing that it would be both safe and memorable. We negotiated, and though I don't recall the specifics, I know it involved ice cream.

It was nearly nine o'clock—go time. We tiptoed through a neighbor's yard and stopped in the bushes by the porch of our friends' home. I could feel my father approving every comical step and giddy giggle.

I channeled my inner Vince Lombardi and gave my pint-sized team a short pep talk. They listened and nodded at the right times, but I suspect they knew the speech was more for me than for them.

I stepped up on the porch and set the heavy jar on the welcome mat. I'd included a short, typed note that explained the purpose of the jar and why they'd been selected. It was as vague as it could possibly be to protect our identity.

My girls remained in the bushes. "Come up," I whispered. "You don't want to miss this!"

They shook their heads and though their mouths didn't move, their eyes said it all: "Don't push it, pal. We don't want to get caught, or worse, arrested."

Through the years, I've wondered what else they thought in that pivotal moment in family history. All those lectures about safety, respect for private property, using good judgment, not succumbing to peer pressure—and here I was dragging them into the bushes of a home after dark on Christmas Eve.

I smiled and reached forward to ring the bell—which was covered with a large piece of tape. The universal sign that says, "Don't ring me. I'm broken. You better knock."

"Uh-oh," I said.

But I knocked.

As I gently rapped on the door, my thoughts started to spin. What if they didn't discover the jar? What if it stayed out all night?

My knocking became louder.

What if they didn't use that door on Christmas day? Would the money be stolen? Would the impact be dimmed if they didn't find it right away? Or ever?

By now I was banging loud enough it could have been an FBI raid. Then I heard footsteps and voices approaching.

"Dad! Dad!" My girls must have thought I'd decided to break in.

I jumped off the porch and began running back toward the spot where my wife was waiting with the getaway car.

Then I realized my accomplices were still in the bushes.

I ran back, scooped them up like sacks of potatoes, and sprinted through several yards. The Honda Odyssey rolled up with the door open.

"Get in!" Kodi shouted.

We sped off at a pace that would have made Jeff Gordon proud. Even NASA was probably impressed.

We got home in a fraction of the time it would normally take and took speed bumps like we were racing RC cars. I'll never forget pulling in the driveway, killing the headlights, and slinking in the house.

We locked the front door behind us, and my daughters shut the drapes that protected our huge, street-facing windows.

Then, they simply fell to the floor and laughed. I knew then that they were feeling something so special, so unique, that they didn't know how to articulate it.

If I could have taken a photo of that moment, it would be my all-time favorite. If I could have filmed it, it would have become one of my life's instant classics.

It was in that moment that I knew I was seeing in my children's eyes what my father probably longed to see in mine and never had.

Absolute charity.

The children didn't care what they got for Christmas the next morning. And clearly, the experience had become the greatest gift my wife and I could have ever received.

My girls were ready to begin another jar immediately. By the next evening, Christmas night, another jar was scrubbed, shined, and dried. We placed it on the counter, and soon our coins again began to accumulate like snowflakes that fall every day of the year.

This thing, this idea, this jar now had a name.

It was our Christmas Jar.

The Novella

As the days piled up, I pondered whether our experience was worth sharing with others. The season and the delivery had changed us.

Christmas—more importantly *Christ*—had become more central than ever to our family's story. I wondered whether our experiment could be fictionalized into a short novella that might inspire another family to do the same.

If one family read it, I thought, *and they did the same experiment, wouldn't it be worth it?*

It began early one morning as a five-page short story. The title changed several times as it grew to ten pages, then twenty pages—then eventually it became *Christmas Jars*.

I wrote before work, during lunch, and after work whenever I could. I wrote at the public library, sneaking in snacks and disappearing to the "quiet room."

If the library was closed, I settled into a back wall booth at IHOP. If they had a writers-in-residence program, I'd be the pancake chairman.

After I'd completed the manuscript, I invited close friends and family to read it and offer brutally honest feedback. One of my brothers, Jeff, has an eagle eye for typos and was especially helpful in polishing the story from a gawky rough draft to something ready for prom.

Mostly, I asked these early readers to consider whether the story would inspire them to start their own Christmas Jar.

Weeks later, I realized that I'd never really know if the little manuscript had potential until I circulated it beyond folks with the same last name as mine and who might feel an obligation to tell me how wonderful it is.

(This is especially true of mothers. If I wrote a haiku on the back of a Twinkie wrapper, my mother would tell me that it was destined to be an international bestseller.)

I remember the Sunday morning I first sent it off to someone I didn't know. I'd posted a message to an online newsgroup that I had a short Christmas-themed manuscript, and I was looking for feedback. I offered to send a PDF file to anyone interested and was surprised at the lightning-quick replies. I had six requests before I'd even taken a breath.

I nervously attached the document and added a few lines of instruction. I was sincerely looking for their unfiltered, unbiased feedback. Off the manuscript went into cyberspace, and off we went to church.

By the time we returned hours later, I already had my first response. I didn't recognize her name, and to this day, we've never met. But her reaction to the manuscript was the turning point that suggested my life was about to change.

> Thank you, thank you for letting me read this. I am crying as I write this. It was very moving, what a great message of random acts of kindness. Let me know when it is published. I would like to buy a copy.
> Contact me again when your next project is ready.
> Shelley in Nova Scotia

Before we were done, approximately one hundred people had requested and read the manuscript. They found typos I'd overlooked a dozen times, but the reaction was overwhelmingly positive.

I wanted to hug them all. My next step, according to all the writing websites, was to find an agent who would represent the book. I selected twenty and sent the manuscript.

Agent by agent, it was rejected, including by Laurie Liss, the woman who'd always been my dream agent. She represented other authors in my genre, and I thought if the book had a chance, she just might be the one to give it that chance.

To her great credit, she sent me a personalized, kind reply telling me that the market was tight for Christmas novellas. She wished me well, and unlike most of the other rejections, it was not a form letter.

Another rejection stood out for the wrong reasons. A well-known agent told me that she loved the concept; she only wished someone else had written it.

I considered giving her phone number to my mom.

With twenty rejections under my belt, I was prepared to head down to the local copy shop, make a few comb-bound copies for friends and family, and call it good. I still had hope that someone would read my homemade book and turn it into a family tradition.

My wife had other ideas, as she usually does, and they were better than mine, as they usually are.

She encouraged me to bypass agents and send it directly to publishers. I knew there were a few that still accepted unagented, unsolicited manuscripts, and I gave it a shot. To my surprise, all three publishers I approached expressed interest.

One, Shadow Mountain, moved more quickly than the others, and I was staring at a contract within days.

Like the night my family delivered that pioneer jar, I remember my first call with editor Chris Schoebinger like it happened this morning. Schoebinger is a creative genius who probably deserves more credit than anyone else for this book still being relevant a decade later.

Pacing around my bedroom, I listened as he laid out a marketing strategy and wowed me with big numbers and bigger expectations. When he offered me a small advance, I nearly dropped the phone.

That was April 2005, and the next one hundred days were a whirlwind.

On another call, not long after we made the deal, I was back pacing in my bedroom when I posed the question that keeps every publisher and author awake at night: How many books do you *really* think we can sell?

Schoebinger paused and, in a tone that said he wasn't just convincing me, suggested that he thought they could sell 20,000 copies without much of a major marketing push.

After we hung up, I found my wife downstairs, and she asked how it went.

"Well, I think that guy's gonna lose his job," I said, one-quarter kidding.

As the months passed, Schoebinger revealed increasing optimism that the book had potential to surprise.

I remember where I was when he said they were estimating a first print run of 40,000.

I remember where I was when he said the number had risen to 50,000.

I was on vacation in late summer in Baker City, Oregon, when Schoebinger called and dropped a memorable bomb.

He explained that even some grocery stores were interested in carrying the book, so they were now up to an estimate of 80,000 copies.

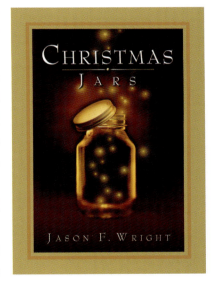

If one of my kids had flown off a metal merry-go-round at a park right then, I wouldn't have noticed.

Back in Virginia a few weeks later, I took a break from a long day of work and went for a walk around our neighborhood. I was heading for home when I got a call from Angie Godfrey. She worked for the publisher in marketing and had quickly become one of my very favorite people.

(In fact, though she no longer works there and hasn't for many years, we remain dear friends.)

She was calling about another matter, but before we hung up, I asked how production was coming. Because I was a complete unknown as an author and there were maybe seven people waiting for the book to release, the publisher had not set a "strict on sale" date.

That meant stores would be permitted to shelve a book whenever it arrived, so stores might have it days or weeks before others.

"So, the books are probably in your warehouse by now?"

"They should be. I can actually pull that up on my computer. Hold on."

I slowed my pace and listened.

"Wow," she said. "That's a lot of books."

"How many?"

"88,000."

I nearly ran home. I shared the print run number with my wife and once again added my voice of warning about my editor. "He's going to need a Christmas Jar of his own when this thing is over."

Before long the book was out and, like most authors, I remember going in and buying it for the first time. I paid with my debit card and secretly hoped that the clerk at Barnes & Noble would notice.

She didn't.

But I smiled anyway when she slipped the book into a bag with the receipt.

The weeks leading up to Christmas were a rush in every way. Several national radio and television shows had mentioned the book and I was getting more direct orders on my website than I could ship. I spent days hunting down books from every store I could find and calling in favors I had not earned. My family lived in my kitchen as I personally signed, hand-addressed, and shipped thousands of books.

It was three things: thrilling, exhausting, and the kind of mistake you only make once.

By December 15, the book was impossible to find, and though I didn't know it, the seeds of a movement had been planted.

Royalties and Pins

Another milestone memory came when I received my first royalty check. I like to say that it wasn't enough to change our lives, and that's true, but it was enough to go to Wendy's and go "Biggie."

"Frostys!" I told the kids, and there was much squealing heard throughout the land. Some of it even came from them.

As I studied that check, and I do mean *studied* it, I relished the fact that my name was on the front. *This is mine!* I thought. And I didn't mean the royalties, but the whole shebang.

My wife likes to think that I'm a balloon and she's a pin. She likes to imagine this because it's true.

With my head expanding and my pride on ice cream steroids, she looked across the room and held up that figurative pin.

"Pop."

I knew what was coming.

"You know that doesn't belong to you, right?"

"The check?" I laughed. "I beg to differ. It has my name on it."

"No, I mean the book."

"Umm. It has my name on it, too."

She sighed, because that's what she does when she's right. And she's almost always right.

Fine, she's *always* right.

"No, I mean this whole thing. All of it. You were the one inspired to write it, but it belongs to all the people who are reading the book and taking the challenge."

I nodded politely, but it was hard to concentrate when I was holding the check like a mother holds her son at the airport.

"This belongs to God, in a way. You were just telling His story. You're blessed it was you, we're blessed, but it's not *ours*."

In time, the conversation waned, and I made my way to bed. I would have patted her on the head when I walked by her on the couch, but writers need their hands.

She doesn't get it, I thought.

Naturally, I soon realized that *I* was the one who didn't get it.

Back to the Beginning

So. I'm sitting at my computer in the early morning hours of December 26, 2005. We're living in a shoebox home in Fairfax, Virginia, and my two daughters and baby boy are tucked away in happy slumber.

The novel had blessed our lives in ways I'd never imagined, and I was already brainstorming my next novel, *The Wednesday Letters*, a book I'd been writing in my head for years.

Then it came, that email that launched a thousand more.

> On Christmas Eve this year, I received an unmarked box on my front doorstep. Inside was a mason jar full of bills and coins. It was simply marked in red and green letters as the "Christmas Jar." Included in the box was a plain wrapped gift. I frantically tore open the gift hoping to find some clue as to the intent of the jar, and found Jason Wright's book, *The Christmas Jar*.
>
> Quickly I scanned through its cover to find a summarized description of the book, and the reason behind the gifts. If I wasn't on medication to prevent me from crying, I would have been shedding those tears aplenty as I counted the money. Inside the center of the single one-dollar bills was a hidden one-hundred dollar bill.
>
> I felt like a starving street person as I scrounged and sorted the coins. I added up a total of $158.71.
>
> I am a 47-year-old single parent of two, and have been for greater than 17 years. I don't receive assistance. I work. I am the percentage that makes more than what is needed to qualify, but still the income is only enough to pay the bills.
>
> I'm unable to finish my story, it has been difficult to explain.

Suffice it to say, I would not have been able to buy any presents for my kids without the money in the jar, and I thank Mr. Wright's book for the inspiration that encouraged some friend of mine to help me. And honestly, I thank God, because he does hear our prayers, and always provides me with just exactly what I need!

SHERRI D.

Tears filled my eyes. Soon, they spilled onto my cheeks, and I knew there was no point in wiping them until the wave passed.

I immediately forwarded the email to my wife, mother, and siblings. "Can you believe it?"

Over the next several weeks, that single story became two, then four, and then a dozen. We've seen lives transformed forever by the miracle of the right jar going to the right family at the right time.

We've seen prayers answered by a knock at the door at the very moment hope was hanging by a silver piece of tiny, tired tinsel.

We've seen children smile and parents cry because those rehearsed conversations about how "Santa got lost" never had to happen.

A young cancer patient named Cameron Birch was given two giant jars that same Christmas Eve and refused to keep a penny from either one. Instead, he asked to use the money to buy toys, puzzles, and books for the playroom at the cancer center where he spent so much of his time.

Cameron died in February, but all these years later, the tradition lives on in that boy's home. His family has given away a jar every year since.

I had the honor of meeting that Christmas Jar pioneer a few days before he died. Sitting at the side of his hospital bed in his humble living room, I finally realized what Kodi had meant that night when she said the words that blew past me.

"This doesn't belong to *you*."

She was right.

The book, the tradition, and the spirit of the jar belongs to Cameron, Sherri, and all the others who've given or received a jar.

After that crucial pivot point, eager to hear more of the stories being written on dark porches, in church pews, and in parking lots, I began inviting people to share their experiences at www.christmasjars.com.

I called them submissions, then stories, and then gravitated to the word that best fit: *miracles*.

If you thought I shed tears after that first email, imagine the emotions in the decade since.

The Next Chapter

A lot has unfolded in the years since that first Christmas Jar. Most importantly, people who know math better than I do—which includes everyone reading this book, all children, and most pets—estimate the global Christmas Jars family has given away nearly $15 million in clean quarters and dirty dimes.

That's a lot of couch cushion and cup holder change.

My career has changed too. After all those promises I made to my mother, my wife, and God that I'd become a writer when I grew up, I grew up.

At least on paper.

I've written twenty more books with several more in the literary oven. I've written middle-grade fiction, biographies, dabbled in ghostwriting, and been published on hundreds of websites and in traditional newspapers across the country.

I've also spoken to corporate, church, and nonprofit groups large and small in nearly every state and presented assemblies and workshops to hundreds of thousands of K–12 students. Confession? My favorite part of being a writer isn't the writing. It's looking in the dreaming eyes of a young student and telling them that no matter what life throws their way, I will always believe in them.

Because that's exactly what my teachers said to me.

What else? My Kindness Card movement has "become a thing"—as my kids would say. I've talked about it on many local and national shows like *GMA3* and *The Kelly Clarkson Show*.

I've branched into podcasting and publicity and have helped other writers finish, publish, and publicize their own books.

Christmas Jars—The Movie was finally released in 2019 and introduced a new generation to the movement. Our partners Muse Studio and BYUtv did such a terrific job, and I'm not afraid to say that unlike many adaptations, the film might be better than the book!

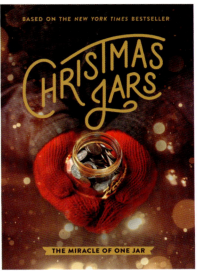

Other books of mine, including *The Wednesday Letters*, *The Seventeen Second Miracle*, and *Even the Dog Knows* are also in various stages of film development. I spend time every single day chasing opportunities and relationships to get those made.

Despite the other books, the movies, and countless other ideas—some good, some awful—nothing will replace the magic of the Christmas Jar movement.

During the first few years after its publication, I wondered if I'd ever be known for anything other than the little novella someone once said was so short, it should have been shelved with the pamphlets.

No matter what else I wrote, people asked me about the book, the jars, and the tradition. *What a curse*, I thought.

Even now, at every stop, every signing, and every interview, I'm asked about that really little book with really long legs. Recently, an independent bookstore owner asked me at the end of an event, "Does it bother you that *Christmas Jars* is still your bestselling book?"

Countless coins and miracles later, I humbly answer, "Not at all. What a blessing."

Indeed. What a miracle that a book that came from a family experiment has turned into a tradition that changes lives and answers prayers.

As my wise wife said a decade ago in our quiet living room, this doesn't belong to me anyway. It never has.

It belongs to every single person who has been touched by the magic of a jar.

What started as a tiny tradition in our small family has grown into a massive movement in a family that will never stop growing.

Will you join us?

CHRISTMAS JARS

JOURNAL

Our name _____

Year _____

The family or person we chose: _____

Why we chose them: _____

_____

_____

_____

_____

What happened with our Christmas Jar delivery: _____

_____

_____

_____

_____

_____

_____

_____

_____

_____

_____

_____

_____

Our name _____

Year _____

The family or person we chose: _____

Why we chose them: _____

_____

_____

_____

_____

What happened with our Christmas Jar delivery: _____

_____

_____

_____

_____

_____

_____

_____

_____

_____

_____

_____

_____

Our name _____

Year _____

The family or person we chose: _____

Why we chose them: _____

_____

_____

_____

_____

What happened with our Christmas Jar delivery: _____

_____

_____

_____

_____

_____

_____

_____

_____

_____

_____

_____

_____

Our name _____

Year _____

The family or person we chose: _____

Why we chose them: _____

_____

_____

_____

_____

What happened with our Christmas Jar delivery: _____

_____

_____

_____

_____

_____

_____

_____

_____

_____

_____

_____

_____

Our name _____

Year _____

The family or person we chose: _____

Why we chose them: _____

_____

_____

_____

_____

What happened with our Christmas Jar delivery: _____

_____

_____

_____

_____

_____

_____

_____

_____

_____

_____

_____

_____

Our name _____

Year _____

The family or person we chose: _____

Why we chose them: _____

_____

_____

_____

_____

What happened with our Christmas Jar delivery: _____

_____

_____

_____

_____

_____

_____

_____

_____

_____

_____

_____

Our name _____

Year _____

The family or person we chose: _____

Why we chose them: _____

_____

_____

_____

_____

What happened with our Christmas Jar delivery: _____

_____

_____

_____

_____

_____

_____

_____

_____

_____

_____

_____

Our name _____

Year _____

The family or person we chose: _____

Why we chose them: _____

_____

_____

_____

_____

What happened with our Christmas Jar delivery: _____

_____

_____

_____

_____

_____

_____

_____

_____

_____

_____

_____

_____

Acknowledgments

If you're actually reading the acknowledgments, you have either made and given away everything in the book, or you're in the dentist's chair waiting for your decennial teeth cleaning. In either case, we're proud of you.

Much like the recipes and crafts in these pages, this book itself came together through carefully curated ingredients and a highly scientific, lab-tested process.

If you'd like to publish your own cook- and craft-book someday, we suggest the following recipe:

INGREDIENTS

1 Editorial Crew—Heidi Gordon, Callie Hansen, Derk Koldewyn

1 Marketing Team—Amy Parker, Troy Butcher, Hailey Haskins, Lehi Quiroz

1 Designer—Heather Ward

1 Agent—Claudia Cross

1 Team of Business Partners—you know who you are, why you matter, and how thankful we are for your faith

1 Family—Oakli and Troy, Gary, Annie, Shane, Charlie, Jadi, Kason, Koleson, Beverly, Sandi, Gayle, Sterling and Ann, Jeff and April, Terilynne and John

1 Christmas Jars Community—please insert your name here. (Yes, that means you. The dentist will wait.)

INSTRUCTIONS

Take all ingredients except marketing and mix them in a figurative industrial-sized creative blender.

Slowly stir in the marketing team last; they like to see what they're working with.

Blend for twenty years or until the screaming stops, whichever comes first.

Spread the mixture onto a nonstick baking sheet that's exactly the size of this cookbook.

Bake for 7–11 minutes on a four-color press.

Add cover.

Delivery tip: Be sure to purchase and deliver a copy to friends, family, neighbors, coworkers, church leaders, choir directors, librarians, pest control service providers, anyone named Nate, and, of course, your dentist.

For more information or to share your Christmas Jar miracle,
visit www.christmasjars.com.

For more information about the author, visit www.jasonfwright.com.

INDEX